Making Your Own
WINE
at HOME

Making Your Own
WINE
at HOME

Creative Recipes for Making Grape, Fruit, and Herb Wines

LORI STAHL

FOX CHAPEL
PUBLISHING

ISBN 978-1-56523-826-8

All photography by Lori Stahl unless otherwise noted.

Library of Congress Cataloging-in-Publication Data
Stahl, Lori.
 Making your own wine at home / Lori Stahl.
     pages cm
 Includes index.
 ISBN 978-1-56523-826-8
 1. Wines and winemaking--Amateurs' manuals. I. Title.
 TP548.2.S74 2014
 641.87'2--dc23
                 2014008667

To learn more about the other great books from Fox Chapel Publishing, or to find a retailer near you,
call toll-free 800-457-9112 or visit us at *www.FoxChapelPublishing.com*.

Note to Authors: We are always looking for talented authors to write new books. Please send a brief letter describing your idea to Acquisition Editor, 1970 Broad Street, East Petersburg, PA 17520.

Printed in China
First printing

Acquisition editor
Peg Couch

Copy editor
Colleen Dorsey

Cover and layout designer
Jason Deller

Developmental editor
Ayleen Stellhorn

Editor
Colleen Dorsey

Dedication

This book is dedicated to Jim and Sandy Witmyer:
My appreciation for sharing Coopers Hill Farm with me and the wisdom, bounty, and insights the two of you cultivated in your vineyard and wine supply business there. A sincere wish that this book will nurture winemakers as you have nurtured me.

This book is also dedicated to Katie Stahl:
For being you and for enduring life in the fray of a mom whose winemaking transformed your home into a wine lab.

INTRODUCTION

This book is meant to serve as an invitation to and a companion for someone who has never made wine before and, perhaps, as a liberating inspiration to someone who has. If you are anything like I was, a curiosity and intrigue about this ancient art has grown insatiable, and adding yeast to your first batch of wine is inevitable. I've written this book to hopefully give you the freedom to play at winemaking.

First, we will explore common tools, equipment, and ingredients used in winemaking. We will go through the steps of creating wine from a kit, then a concentrate. From there we will begin to jazz it up a bit, first adding fruit to a concentrate, then on to making wine from grapes, fruit, and even flowers and herbs. I'll encourage suggestions of ways to mix it up, and I'll share a few tales of wine-related adventures. We will visit markets, orchards, and an Amish lady's backyard in our quest for fruit. I've tried to photograph as much as I could along the way, and yes, my camera did end up a little sticky, as I reached for it all too often amid fruit picking, grape crushing, and at every step of the process.

I hope to convey a bit of what was revealed to me of the rhythm of winemaking and tuning into the cycles of fermentation and of nature. I'll share every tip I've discovered and even confess to some amusing blunders. I'll encourage that you create a community to share in your winemaking and your wine. I'll offer new twists on traditional recipes and sweet ways to enjoy, appreciate, and indulge in the wines you have created.

I hope this book encourages you to take the first steps on what has been a very enjoyable path for me, and I hope the first time you uncork your very first batch of wine, the aroma delights you and the liquid reveals to you the essence of that which you have fermented.

CONTENTS

Creative Ingredients for Delicious Wine

Get your adventure in winemaking started with the diverse array of recipes inside this book. You'll get the straight scoop on how to make wines from kits, concentrates, fresh fruit, and beyond. Whether your taste is Chardonnay, Riesling, or a funky fruit wine, you'll love trying your hand at the 29 amazing recipes found in these pages.

Chapter 1
GETTING STARTED

Read up on the basics before you jump into winemaking to ensure your success and save you time and money. In this chapter, you'll learn about winemaking equipment, essential and optional ingredients, typical winemaking techniques, and how to bottle, store, and label your finished masterpieces. You'll also get a special look at growing your own ingredients and meet five talented people—farmers, suppliers, chemists, and artists—who have worked some aspect of winemaking into their lives.

EQUIPMENT

First, you must familiarize yourself with some of the terminology, equipment, and ingredients used in winemaking. This may seem daunting, but fear not; a few basics are all you need to get started.

The basic equipment you'll need for making wine is simple:

- Bucket (to start your wine in, called a primary fermenter)
- Jug (to finish your wine in, called a carboy or secondary fermenter)
- Bottles and corks (to store your finished wine)
- Clear tubing (a way to move your wine from container to container)
- Airlock with bung (to protect your wine during fermentation)
- Thermometer (very useful during fermentation)
- Hydrometer (also useful during fermentation)

Equipment for home winemaking can be easily found and is not too expensive.

From left to right, back row: 5-gallon carboy, 6-gallon carboy, 3-gallon carboy; front row: 1-gallon jug/ secondary fermenter, ½-gallon jug/secondary fermenter.

As you delve deeper into home winemaking, you'll want to acquire other helpful tools, including a scale, measuring spoons that include a ⅛ teaspoon (0.5mL), straining bags, a long stirring spoon, and a drill attachment with paddles. Other kitchen tools that can multitask for winemaking include potato mashers, measuring cups, and, of course, bottles, corks, corkscrews, and all sorts of clever tools for decanting and serving wine (more on that in chapter 4, Enjoying Your Wine). Another useful tool is a heating pad. This unlikely tool can be really helpful if your winemaking space is not at an optimal temperature. On many a cold winter's night I've tucked one between two primary fermenters to help the yeast get off to a good start. As you progress in your winemaking, you should also add acid and pH test kits and filtration systems to your stash of tools.

Descriptions of common winemaking equipment follow. Some of these items will make more sense after you've read and understood the winemaking techniques. Refer back to this section as needed.

Winemaker's journal

One of the most important pieces of winemaking equipment is the tablet, notebook, or journal that you dedicate to your winemaking activities. Write down information about your ingredients, your equipment, your successes, and your failures. Include anything that will help you improve your next batch.

Primary fermenter

A primary fermenter is a vessel in which a batch of wine is started. Most commonly used is a 6-gallon (22.7L) bucket made of a special food-grade plastic with markings on the side to denote fill levels and a plastic lid with a small rubber gasketed hole for an airlock. You can also use a glass primary fermenter (or "primary" for short), but this will change how you should set up the primary. As the yeast consumes the sugars, they are converted into alcohol and carbon dioxide. The carbon dioxide needs somewhere to go; if you were to seal a primary fermenter tightly, eventually the pressure would build up such that the primary would most likely explode and make a mess. If you are using a bucket as a primary, an airlock will fit into the rubber gasketed hole, and the gas will escape through that airlock. If you are using a glass jar as a primary, leave the lid slightly askew or prop it open with something to allow the gas to escape. Also, if it is summer, I highly advise using something to cover the entire opening of the primary, because it will attract fruit flies.

Primary fermenter with fill level markings

Secondary fermenter

Use a secondary fermenter to complete the fermentation. Common sizes include a one-gallon (3.8L) jug, and a three-, five-, six-, or thirteen-gallon (11.4, 18.9, 22.7, or 49.2L) carboy (sometimes referred to as a demijohn). These vessels are typically glass; some sizes are available in plastic. See photo on page 14. Wine should never be kept in anything less than a high grade PET plastic carboy made for fermenting. You cannot simply use old milk jugs or water cooler jugs—that plastic is not the appropriate density for alcohol storage and may cause problems or a chemical taste in the wine.

Carboys

Carboys are often used for secondary fermentations. These large containers are most often made of glass or plastic. A tapered top closes to a small spout. See photo on page 14.

Glass primary fermenter, an alternative to plastic

A NOTE ABOUT METRICS

This book includes metric conversions for all measurements, including pounds, fluid ounces, gallons, cups, tablespoons, teaspoons, and inches. Metric equivalents are occasionally rounded for ease of use where the rounding will not interfere with the successful execution of the recipes. Note that some aspects of the recipes are difficult to convert conveniently, such as the use of one-gallon fermenters, which is equivalent to a 3.8L volume, but which is not a commonly available size in countries that utilize the metric system. Adapt the recipes as necessary to suit your tools and abilities. Anyone preparing a recipe from the metric measurements can double check the measurements if needed to ensure best results.

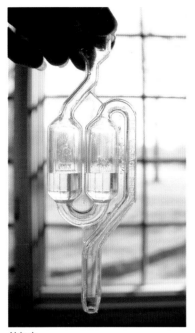

Airlock

A bung and airlock are inserted in the opening of the primary fermenter and provide a way for gas to escape the wine.

Siphon

Airlock

An airlock provides a clever way for gas to be released from the wine by letting it bubble out through a barrier that prevents anything unwanted from entering the wine. Several styles of airlocks are available. The most common are plastic (see photo); I prefer plastic because they show how rapidly the fermentation is bubbling. (I also had a terrible experience when a glass airlock broke, causing shards of glass to fall into my wine.)

Bung

A bung is a rubber stopper with a hole for an airlock that is inserted into the opening of the primary fermenter.

Auto siphon/siphon tube

The auto siphon/siphon tube moves wine from vessel to vessel. Gravity is your friend in this process, as you'll put the wine you are racking up on a table and the jug you are going into down lower. An auto siphon is pumped; to use a siphon tube you must create suction by sucking on the hose and probably getting a mouthful of whatever you're making. (It's important to note that getting a mouthful is way more fun as wines are finishing than it is early on in a fermentation.) Don't pour the wine between vessels; the splashing introduces too much oxygen into the process.

Thermometer

A thermometer is very important to monitor temperature throughout the winemaking process. Wine thermometers float. I like to use an 8" (20cm) glass thermometer, which is inexpensive and comes in handy at many points in the process.

Hydrometer

A hydrometer is a gauge that can help guide you in your fermentations and help calculate the alcohol in your wine. It's not strictly necessary when you are just starting out with kits.

Corker

A corker is a device that puts a cork in a bottle. I'd highly advise getting a floor model because the handheld ones can be tricky to work with. This piece of equipment is easily shared if you have other winemaking friends.

Bottle filler

A bottle filler attaches to the siphon tube and is used when bottling your wine; it's an important tool to have because you do not want your wine to splash and get oxidized when going into the bottle. It lets wine flow when you push down on it, releasing a stop valve.

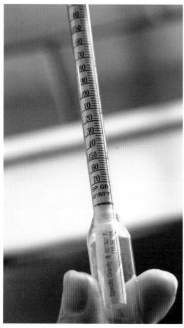

Hydrometer

Corker

Bottle filler

Crusher

Wine press

Bottle tree (a bottle washer)

Wine thief

A wine thief is a clever little gadget that allows you to dip it into a carboy and pull out a small volume of wine to use for testing (and tasting—but try to resist, as you'll need to keep things topped up).

Crusher

A crusher is used to crush and take stems out of grapes. Crushers can be anything from a simple tabletop hand-cranked machine to a large, elaborate motorized wizard. The original "crusher" was the classic people walking on the grapes with their feet; you can also do your crushing by hand. Crushers are expensive, but do come in handy if you are processing large quantities of grapes.

Press

A press is used to extract every bit of goodness out of grapes. When choosing a press, larger may not be better unless you plan to work with large quantities of grapes. Purchase a press directly from a wine supply store to avoid costly shipping expenses.

Refractometer

A refractometer is used to measure the brix (amount of sugar) in grapes. It helps to decide when to harvest grapes and how to handle initial fermentation decisions.

Bottle washers

Bottle washers and bottle draining stands come in a variety of shapes and sizes and can be very helpful, as sanitation is key in winemaking.

Bottle cleaning funnel

Bottle cleaning brush

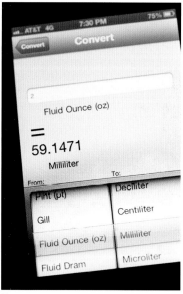

Phone apps

Strainer

Bottle cleaners

Bottle cleaning tools such as a bottle brush or a funnel with tiny stainless steel ball bearings are used to get tough stains from hard to reach places in bottles and carboys. You may want to have a few sizes of brushes on hand: smaller ones for wine bottles and a larger one with a band for carboys.

Apps

Some great apps out there are ultra helpful with the task of making conversions. (In my winemaking, it seems that I am forever making conversions!)

Straining tools

Straining is a big part of winemaking. Straining bags are often used by winemakers to keep fruit contained during fermentations and to make it easier to transfer wine from the primary to the secondary fermenter. Personally, I do not use them often in my recipes, simply because I make an absurd number of batches of wine and I'm seldom, if ever, in any kind of a hurry for my wines. I do find it very helpful to squeeze any citrus needed in winemaking recipes over a strainer to keep the juice free of seeds and pulp. Some great funnels on the market have strainers built into them, saving you a step.

INGREDIENTS

Here you'll learn all of the essential winemaking ingredients. Read them over now so that you are ready when you tackle the recipes.

Fruit

Fruit should be of fine quality and very ripe but still in great shape. If there are any bad spots, cut them off before winemaking. You can use fresh, frozen, canned, and dried fruits. Fresh is typically best, but in midwinter, anything goes. Freezing can actually be better for some fruits, since it breaks the fruit down, releasing more juice, but it's best to freeze your own rather than buy frozen. Try freezing berries and some grapes.

Use the fruit of your choice.

Flowers and herbs are a creative ingredient.

Flowers and herbs

Flowers and herbs can be lovely additions to or the dominant ingredient in wines. We'll learn more about this in the recipe section.

Water

Spring water is always a safe bet; never use distilled or deionized water. Water can add flavor, so the area you live in will determine whether you can use well water or treated municipal tap water. In some areas well water has high mineral content that can ruin the taste of the wine. Similarly, in some areas the municipal water is highly chlorinated, so you may want to let it stand overnight to allow the chlorine to dissipate; but not all municipalities chlorinate their water to the point that you need to let it stand. Be aware that letting water stand does offer an opportunity for bacteria to infect it.

Sugar

Sugar feeds the yeast and is converted to alcohol. One of the very best types of pure cane sugar to use in winemaking is the traditional white sugar. There are many other types of sweeteners that can be fermented: agave, honey, maple, brown sugar, brown rice syrup, and malt. For the recipes in this book, I advise pure cane sugar.

Sugar feeds the yeast and is converted into alcohol.

The ingredients in wine go beyond good fruit. You will also need various nutrients, yeasts, tablets, and other additives.

Yeast

Yeast is what makes the magic happen: fermentation. There are many kinds and brands of yeast available, and most come in small 2 oz. (5g) packets. We will learn more about using yeast as we get into the examples and recipes.

Hydrating yeast

Campden tablets

Campden tablets are a very easy way to add sulfite, especially in small wine batches that only need very small quantities of sulfite. Early on, sulfite serves to kill unwanted natural yeast and bacteria, and later in the process serves as a preservative.

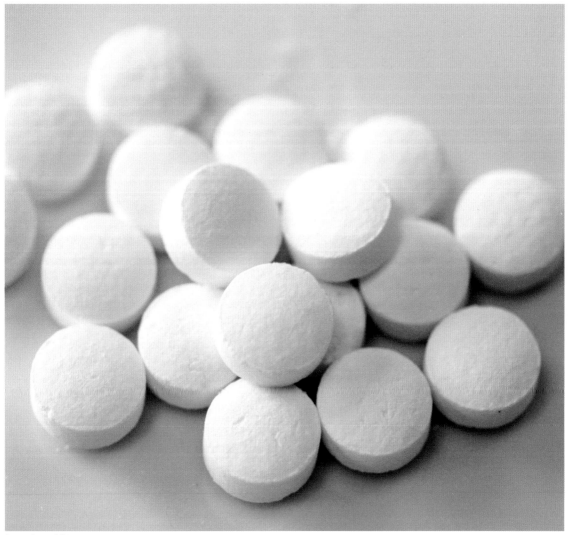

Campden tablets

Additives and Their Uses

The following, less obvious ingredients used in winemaking are often just as important as the main ingredients. Purchase additives like the ones described in the chart following in small quantities, and be sure to store them in an airtight container.

Additives are usually grains or powders.

Additive	Uses	Components
Potassium metabisulfite	Potassium, or sodium, metabisulfite is used in cleaning, as a preservative, and to kill wild yeast. Potassium is preferred over sodium for preserving your wine. Use extreme care when working with this chemical. When possible, work outside when measuring. You do not want to take in a strong whiff of this; it is nasty stuff. Take the time to look up the Material Safety Data Sheet (otherwise known as the MSDS) for it and familiarize yourself with recommended handling procedures.	—
Acid	Acid is used in most fruit wine recipes. It influences color, balance, and taste and gives a crisp tartness; without it, wines can taste flat. Acid also helps yeast during fermentation and protects wine from bacteria.	Older wine recipes often specified one type of acid. Most modern recipes call for acid blend, which is a combination of citric, tartaric, and malic acids.

Additive	Uses	Components
Tannin	Tannin is added to some wines to increase flavor (it adds zest) and to help with clearing and aging. The recipes in this book include amounts for tannin powder. Tannin is found naturally in some fruits, like grapes, persimmon, blueberry, pomegranate, acai berries, and quince. But most fruits lack tannins. There are also wood tannins that dissolve into wine through contact with oak.	—
Yeast nutrient	Yeast nutrient is essentially just what the name says: food for yeast. It contributes nitrogen, which helps wine yeast to reproduce and makes for good, healthy fermentations.	Nutrient often contains food grade urea and diammonium phosphate.
Yeast energizer	Yeast energizer is like yeast nutrient on steroids. (I mean this metaphorically; you are not literally adding steroids!) The energizer contains all sorts of proteins and vitamin B1 to benefit the yeast and boost fermentation.	Energizer often contains diammonium phosphate, springcell, and magnesium sulphate.
Pectic enzyme	Pectic enzyme is ultra helpful to the fruit winemaking process. The recipes in this book call for a powdered form of pectic enzyme. When added to crushed fruit, pectic enzyme increases the extraction of body and color from the pulp and allows more of the character of the fruit to be appreciated in the wine. It also helps to clear your wine; without it, wines end up with a hazy, almost milky look about them.	—
Potassium sorbate	Potassium sorbate is also called wine stabilizer. This compound is used in a wine that is still sweet after fermentation or in a wine that you intend to sweeten before bottling (you'll read more about back sweetening under Making Alterations, page 44). It loses effectiveness over time, so consult your local supplier to determine how much to purchase.	—

Oak chunks

Oak chips

Oak

Oak is a fabulous winemaking ingredient. Oak stabilizes the wine's color and softens and rounds out the wine's overall character. Oak is available in various forms from various places. The three main countries of origin for winemaking oak are the United States, France, and Eastern Europe/Hungary. Oak comes in powders, small chips, chunks, and even in wood sticks and larger pieces with lots of perforations called staves. The amount of toasting oak receives will impact flavor immensely. Just a word of caution: that old adage "too much of a good thing" definitely applies to oak.

Wine conditioner

Wine conditioner is used to sweeten finished wine. You can add a little to reduce harshness and take a dry edge off, or you can add more to sweeten the wine to taste. Be sure to add potassium sorbate with wine conditioner to prevent refermentation.

As an alternative, you can create your own wine sweetener. Make a simple syrup by boiling one part water with two parts sugar for five minutes. After it cools, you can sweeten the wine according to taste after you've added potassium sorbate. Using a wine conditioner is a safe way to sweeten finished wines.

Meet the Supplier
~ THE WITMYERS ~

Hopefully you are within close proximity of a shop that caters to winemakers. I live just a few miles from Jim and Sandy Witmyer, who supply their local winemaking community with not only grapes, but also many other ingredients and some of the essential equipment that you've learned about so far.

The Witmyers never set out with the intention to start a wine supply business. They planted the first section of their vineyard in 1973 with the intention of growing grapes to sell to wineries. After a few years of struggling to get paid and having prices manipulated by a very big name winery in New York State, the Witmyers decided to put a sign out by the road that said "grapes for sale"—and sell grapes they did. Jim was amazed at the way they had completely underestimated the home winemakers' interest; demand was huge. At first, they just sold grapes, but before you could say "fermentation," the pair were teaching classes in winemaking, and people were asking winemaking advice and needing a packet of yeast for starting their wine and this or that. The Witmyers recognized an opportunity, and they set out to get people what they needed. They quickly grew a full-fledged winemaking supply business.

The community of winemakers that the Witmyers has worked with is a diverse group of wonderful people. Sandy tells some hilarious stories along the way, her favorite being the frequently misunderstood hydrometer reading of zero that causes people to call and complain that their kit resulted in no alcohol (when the reading really means that fermentation is finished and there definitely is alcohol!). Reflecting back on the last forty years, the Witmyers say, "We learned a lot and met a lot of people." I, for one, sure am glad I met them, and I suspect there are a whole lot of other winemakers out there who were helped on their way, too, and feel the exact same way!

▶ Jim and Sandy Witmyer live in southeastern Pennsylvania and run a privately-owned winemaking supply store that is an integral part of the local winemaking community. With experience in everything from pruning (top) to harvesting (middle) to brewing (bottom), they offer essential advice and products.

GROW YOUR OWN

Green thumb or not, if you've got a place to grow things, I highly advise that you do!
Berries, fruit trees, grapes, flowers, and herbs are all fodder for the creative winemaker.
Let's take a closer look at some of the amazing ingredients that you can nurture, harvest,
and turn into amazing wine—all on your own bit of land. After learning about the
ingredients, take a tour through photos of the plants themselves and learn to recognize
them and some of their various growth stages.

Elderberries

Planting elderberries has yielded me both gorgeous elderflowers and elderberries that have
enhanced many a batch of wine. Renowned throughout the world for many centuries for
medicinal purposes, I always hope some of that magic is imparted into my finished wines.

Grapes

Grapes leaves are almost as exciting as the vine's fruit. I enjoy watching them unfurl,
tinged with magenta, then turn a lovely green with hard green berries that ripen to a
beautiful deep purple.

Raspberries

Tending raspberries requires a suit of armor—or, at the very least, some sturdy gloves and
an old sweatshirt. No matter how careful you are, raspberries find a way to stick it to you.

Red Currants

Red currants are bushy plants with sweet little delicate flowers that morph into hard, little
green berries that eventually yield a brilliant red fruit.

Rhubarb

Bountiful rhubarb has a beautiful flavor, but know that its leaves are highly poisonous.
It is a diuretic (acts as a laxative) and has anti-inflammatory properties. Rhubarb must
be cooked; it is inedible raw. Rhubarb also freezes well in stalks or cut up into pieces.

Strawberries

Great varieties of strawberries for winemaking include Albritton, Alpine (shown on
page 33), Cardinal, Dunlap, Earliglow, Empire, Fletcher, Sparkle, Sweet Charlie, and
Purple Wonder. When I can find wild strawberries, I like to add those in the mix, too.
They have an intense flavor that deepens the wine.

Wineberries

Wineberries grow wild in many places. The name says it all!

Weeds

I'm forever roaming about my various gardens, pulling a weed here and there and grabbing
beautiful little handfuls to enhance my cooking and my winemaking. Try it!

Elderberries have long been added to grape wines to improve the richness of red wine color. You can mix elderberry wine with grape wine or mix elderberries with the grapes when preparing the wine.

GRAPES

Grapes are, of course, a challenge and a process to grow, but it can be very rewarding to grow your own. (More information on grape wines on page 106.)

RASPBERRIES

Raspberry wine is fairly intense, and it may need back sweetening, but the flavor is impressive. (Recipe on page 144.)

Pure red currant wine can be delightfully tart; try mixing red currants with raspberries for a light, fresh wine. (Recipe on page 102.)

RHUBARB

Rhubarb is a great addition to strawberry sangria. (Recipe on page 150.)

Strawberries add a summery flavor to any wine. Decide whether you want to leave the seeds in or strain them out, as it could affect the flavor. (Recipe on page 146.)

Wineberries make a red wine similar to a blackberry or raspberry wine, and can be substituted or mixed in blackberry or raspberry recipes. (Recipes on pages 94 and 144.)

WEEDS, NATURE'S BOUNTY

Since weeds are often thought of as a nuisance, not many people have experimented with them in winemaking. But take a chance, and you may just discover something amazing!

Farmers Growing Their Own
~ ALEX WENGER ~

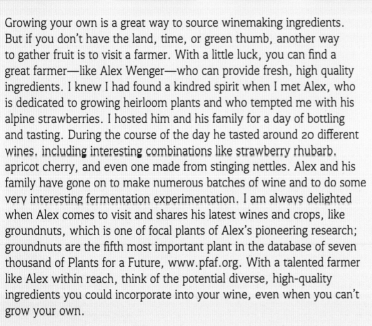

Growing your own is a great way to source winemaking ingredients. But if you don't have the land, time, or green thumb, another way to gather fruit is to visit a farmer. With a little luck, you can find a great farmer—like Alex Wenger—who can provide fresh, high quality ingredients. I knew I had found a kindred spirit when I met Alex, who is dedicated to growing heirloom plants and who tempted me with his alpine strawberries. I hosted him and his family for a day of bottling and tasting. During the course of the day he tasted around 20 different wines, including interesting combinations like strawberry rhubarb, apricot cherry, and even one made from stinging nettles. Alex and his family have gone on to make numerous batches of wine and to do some very interesting fermentation experimentation. I am always delighted when Alex comes to visit and shares his latest wines and crops, like groundnuts, which is one of focal plants of Alex's pioneering research; groundnuts are the fifth most important plant in the database of seven thousand of Plants for a Future, www.pfaf.org. With a talented farmer like Alex within reach, think of the potential diverse, high-quality ingredients you could incorporate into your wine, even when you can't grow your own.

▶ Alex Wenger of Lititz, Pennsylvania has been farming and learning since a very young age on his family's farm, and it shows in his dedication to his work and his expertise in all kinds of ingredients used in winemaking.

TECHNIQUES

In this section we will demystify winemaking and bottling techniques. This is perfect preparation for the next chapter, where you'll learn to make wine step by step; lots of this information will fall into place then.

Note taking

Your wine logbook and your calendar are a perfect starting point to learning about winemaking techniques. Take a look at when steps need to be performed, and be certain that you'll have availability to do the work (timing is more important earlier on in the process). Make very clear notations of your recipe, starting date and time, temperatures, type of yeast, and weights and measures used. Trust me: write it down. You think you'll remember, and then you'll start a few more batches along the way and everything will become a blur.

If you don't take notes as you go, you'll forget useful details about the process.

Choosing a location

One of the first considerations you must address is where you will make your wine. Ideally, your wine should ferment in a dark place. One very important thing to know is that you never want to ferment wine near where you are fermenting other things (like pickles and sauerkraut) as other fermentations can taint the wine. Along those same lines, do not make or store vinegar in the same room where you make wine. Be warned that on occasion fermentations can get out of hand and wine can spew about. Your winemaking area should be easy to clean or well protected against rogue wine.

Temperature is also very important, especially at the start of a fermentation. Maintain a constant temperature of 65 to 70°F (18 to 21°C) unless you are making white wines that benefit from cold fermentation. Remember that the ambient room temperature is not going to be the same as the liquid: fluids usually have a lower temperature than the surrounding air. Yeasts do not like to get cold, and your fermentations will grow sluggish or cease if the temperature gets too cold. Sit a container of water next to what is fermenting and keep a thermometer in it to see what the temperature of the liquid is.

Another, albeit more esoteric, consideration is the energy of the space in which you are doing your winemaking and the energy you bring to your winemaking. I believe the heartfelt love a chef puts into his or her food is reflected and nourishes you immensely; the same goes for a winemaker. Be conscious of the state you are in when you are making wine. Pause, let go of your tensions, and begin with a clear mind and an open heart.

Keeping it all clean

I'll mention over and over again the importance of cleanliness. You must sanitize anything and everything that will come into contact with your wine. Use any cleaners and sanitizers on the market specifically for the home winemaker. Avoid vinegar, bleach, and ammonia. You can also use a diluted solution of potassium metabisulfite (3 to 5 tablespoons [44 to 75mL] to 1 gallon [3.8L] of water). Note that your solution will become weaker over time. Also be sure to clearly label any jug that contains cleaning solution. You don't want to mistake it for water, as a friend of mine once did, and be heartbroken to accidentally pour it directly into whatever you might be making.

Sanitize items that come into contact with anything that comes into contact with the wine. For example, this can opener never touches ingredients directly, but it will touch the rim of the can that contains concentrate. Sanitize it in a sulfite solution. For added precaution, dip a paper towel in sulfite solution and run it around the rim of the can before opening it, for the same reason.

Work hard to keep everything clean using a sulfite solution.

Harvest the best fruits, herbs, and flowers.

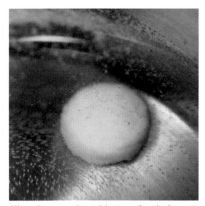
Allow the campden tablet to soften before crushing it.

Rinsing and harvesting ingredients

In the ingredients section, we touched on the importance of using ripe, solid fruit for fermentations. Wash your fruit and prepare it with the same care you would for cooking. I'll give cues in the recipes if things need to be peeled or pitted or cut large or small. Any and all mold, brown spots, and rotting sections must be removed, and underripe fruit should not be used. Do remember if using dried fruits that most have been treated with sulfite and you'll want to wait to add yeast until that has dissipated. The same goes for any flowers or herbs. Harvest them at an optimal time: late morning after the dew has evaporated or before the sun's heat depletes.

Starting your recipe

When starting your recipe by mixing the sugar and water, use warm water, then stir vigorously to dissolve as much of the sugar as possible. If a recipe uses lots of sugar, the yeast can get overwhelmed. Sometimes it can be helpful to either make a yeast starter or to use only part of the sugar and water called for at first, and then add the balance a day or two after a strong fermentation is underway. Make sure that all of the sugar is dissolved before taking a hydrometer reading; otherwise, you may get an inaccurate reading.

We have already talked about the importance of the quality of the water that you use in your winemaking. Be certain that the vessel in which you heat the water has been thoroughly sanitized and rinsed and rinsed again. I tend to heat to just before boiling.

Adding campden

Some people prefer to do their winemaking without the use of chemicals, especially sulfites. My recipes call for sulfite in the form of a campden tablet. Make sure to crush and dissolve the tablet as completely as possible; try adding a solid campden tablet to a small amount of water and let it sit for a minute, as it's easier to crush after it has partially softened. Wait 24 hours before adding yeast so the campden tablet has a chance to kill all the wild yeast and give the yeast you selected the best possible environment in which to grow.

Using a hydrometer

The hydrometer is a great tool to gauge many aspects of fermentation. You'll use it for any one of these tasks:

- Determine the specific gravity of your must (pulp) or wine
- Determine the progress of your fermentation
- Signal when to stop a fermentation; for example, if you want a sweeter wine and do not want to let your wine ferment out to dryness versus back sweetening (see Making Alterations, page 44).
- Estimate the potential alcohol of your batch
- Calculate the percentage of alcohol by comparing your initial reading and your final reading

A hydrometer measures the amount of sugar in the must or wine.

The hydrometer accomplishes all of these tasks by measuring the amount of sugar in a must or wine. The heavier the liquid being tested is, the higher the hydrometer will float. At the beginning of a fermentation, the hydrometer will float at its highest, and at the end, its lowest. This difference in level is because the thick sugars present initially are converted into thin alcohol by the end of the process. Hydrometers contain several scales. We are going to discuss only the specific gravity, the most commonly used scale. The specific gravity of water is 1.000.

You'll want to pull a sample of your must when it is just liquid. Any fruit floating in the sample could impact your reading. A wine thief is a great tool to use for pulling a sample. Many people simply use the tube that their hydrometer came in to take readings, but to ensure cleanliness, it is best to acquire a glass one. To use the hydrometer, first put it in your sample and be sure it is floating freely, then take a reading from the bottom of the meniscus. For most wines you should start with a specific gravity of around 1.090, rack at 1.040, and finish at around 1.000 (1.005 for a sweet wine and 0.990 for a dry wine). A hydrometer is also sensitive to temperature. They are calibrated when they are manufactured to read accurately at a specific temperature (often 60°F [15.5°C]). If your must is at a higher temperature, you will get a slightly low reading. To calculate the alcohol by volume (ABV), take the starting specific gravity and subtract the final specific gravity, then multiply it by 132:

(SG start − SG final) x 132 = ABV

Sample the must as liquid—no floating fruit.

Stir the fermentation to keep the fruit wet.

Punching the cap

It is very important to make sure you "punch down the cap." Typically, early on in a fermentation, your fruit will want to float to the surface. The fruit that is on the very top can dry out or begin to mold if it is not gently stirred under the surface of the liquid. Stir the fermentation twice a day, minimum. Be thorough. Use a sterilized stainless steel potato masher or your hand—your very clean hand—to avoid damaging the fruit.

Growing yeast

The role of yeast in winemaking is paramount. Yeast is truly what makes the magic happen. Through fermentation, yeast converts the sugars into alcohol and carbon dioxide. The more sugar the fruit has, the higher the potential alcohol (if the yeast finishes and converts all the sugar) will be.

The etymology of the word yeast fascinates me. Greek, Sanskrit, German, Welsh... all more or less meant "foams," "froths," "seethes," or "boils." And many a fresh fermentation does indeed exhibit these traits. As a new winemaker, most likely you will experience yeast as little granules (freeze dried yeast culture) that come in a small packet (5 grams, enough to make 5 gallons [18.9L] of wine) that you tear open and sprinkle directly on top of your wine must (do not stir it in!). Alternately, if you choose to hydrate, you tear open the package and, without stirring, gently add to a little water. About 1.7 fluid ounces (50mL) (about ¼ cup) or so of 100 to 105°F (37.78 to 40.55°C) water, well water, or spring water are best (do not use distilled or deionized water!). When hydrated—which ideally takes only a few minutes and 15 minutes at the absolute max—you "pitch," or add to your wine must and stir it in.

This yeast is the catalyst in the alchemy that is winemaking. It quite literally turns the fruit (or fruit and sugar in the case of many fruit wine recipes) into wine.

Some recipes (those higher in sugar) will require a yeast starter, which is simply hydrating the yeast and then giving it a little "snack" before pitching. Think of yeast starters as taking out an insurance policy that your yeast will be off to a good start and that you'll get a strong, complete fermentation.

To create a yeast starter, add a little juice after you hydrate the yeast. People commonly use orange juice—as in, squeeze an orange; do not use a pasteurized, preserved juice because it will inhibit the yeast you are starting. Alternately, you can use some of your must. Just be sure to strain the must you add of any fruit, and don't use must that has just had a sulfite or campden tablet addition. If you just made that addition, wait 8 hours minimum; 24 is better. When creating a yeast starter, essentially you add a little juice, let the yeast multiply a bit, and then add a little more juice. A frothy, foamy, cappuccino-like look atop your starter signals time to pitch. Some people feed their starters for days; I typically feed mine for hours, and so far so good with most of my yeasts "taking off." A yeast starter will also, hopefully, capture more of the delicate flavors and aromas of your fruit as it will have transitioned from freeze-dried particles into functioning yeast that is used to "doing its thing."

Add yeast to warm water or directly to your must.

Do not stir hydrating yeast.

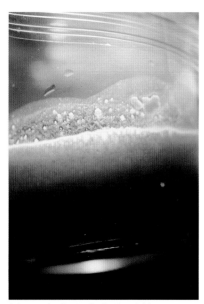
A foamy, frothy top indicates viable yeast.

In addition to ensuring a good fermentation, a starter will indicate if your yeast packet is viable before you add it to your must. If the yeast does not grow and have foam, you will want to secure a fresh, viable packet.

Keep your hydrating yeast, your yeast starter, and your must in a warm place, optimally in a room temperature of 70 to 80°F (21 to 26°C). Ideally, you will be pitching the yeast into a must that is at a similar temperature. Cold is not good to get a yeast started—unless you are using a special cold-tolerant yeast typically employed with white wines.

Grapes and most fruits have natural yeasts in them. Some winemakers brave it and roll with what is naturally present, but it is indeed a risk, and many opt to use a campden tablet to slow or stop the natural yeasts before adding a proven yeast with known positive outcomes. For the beginner home winemaker, this is the best way to go.

Several well-known companies make yeast. Lalvin, Red Star, and White Labs are three big names. I have also had great success working with liquid smack packs from Wyeast. Yeast in this form arrives as a liquid in a foil pouch. You smack the pack to break open a pouch within the pouch, thus activating the yeast. Pitch the yeast when the pack grows swollen. Wyeast is also a source of malolactic cultures, which are most typically added as a secondary fermentation to red wines as they complete their initial fermentation. Those cultures balance and soften the wine and enhance certain flavor and aroma characteristics as they convert malic acid to lactic acid.

The recipes in this book use a Lalvin or Red Star yeast because they are affordable and more commonly available. By all means, understand that this is not in any way the only or even necessarily the best yeast; often several yeasts will meet the desired criteria. Beyond the type of fruit, characteristics of that particular fruit, and the intention to create a sweet or dry wine, consider temperature, alcohol tolerance, and how quickly the yeast carries out a fermentation. Every so often, if you have a stuck fermentation, you'll also need to know where to turn to next.

You can research the properties of a particular yeast online, and you'll find lots of detailed info at:

www.lallemandwine.us/products/yeast_chart.php
www.winemaking.jackkeller.net/strains.asp

Racking your wine

Wines start out with chunks of fruit in what is often a cloudy liquid; things eventually settle out and the liquid itself becomes clearer and clearer. This is when it is time to rack.

Winemakers use the term racking to refer to transferring wine from one vessel to another. When racking, the wine must transfer as gently as possible, without much in the way of splashing, and you must leave behind as much of the sediment that has fallen out of your wine as possible. Place the primary or secondary vessel from which you are racking up high on a table and the jug or carboy into which you are racking down low on the floor. Gravity is your friend, and if the two vessels are at nearly the same height, the racking will take a very long time.

Exercise extreme caution as you begin your siphon. This is one of those situations where I find myself wishing for a third arm. Somehow, just as soon as I get a good flow passing through my siphon tube, the thing comes alive and jumps out of the jug and wine spews forth onto the floor.

Here's a great tip. Before you put the siphon into your jug or carboy, pull the inner chamber up in the air so that the volume of wine that is moved as the siphon enters the jug goes into the siphon and not out over the top and onto your counter (yep, done that a few times, too). Try to keep the bottom of your siphon near the top one-third of the liquid. As the level in the primary fermenter or carboy goes down, very gently tip it on its side so you can get all of the clear liquid on top of what has settled out—or at least as much as possible. Another very important tip is to make sure to clean everything the moment you are finished. Never let your siphon—or hoses or carboys—sit around; it makes cleaning them difficult.

After you have racked your wine, you will often notice that the jug or carboy is no longer filled to the optimal level. The liquid will be about 1" to 1½" (2.5 to 4cm) below the bung, which means you will need to do what winemakers call "top up" with water. Some winemakers will start out with a slightly higher than optimal specific gravity, which will allow for the wine to get watered down when you top up. Some winemakers add sugar to the water they use to top up. Use caution if you make additions, because sometimes the additional sugar can activate the yeast and it does a little volcano thing and erupts out of your carboy. Rack the wine the first time from the primary vessel to the jug or carboy. When you rack the wine additional times for clarity, you will be racking from carboy to carboy or jug to jug.

Tipping the vessel allows the siphon to reach more clear liquid.

Sediment can really pile up at the bottom.

Back sweetening with sugar is an option.

Oak can be added at more than one point during the winemaking process.

Making alterations

There are several things you can do to alter the flavor of your wine.

Back sweetening: If you like and desire a sweet wine, you have two ways to go about making one. You can either halt the fermentation with an addition of potassium sorbate (only recommended for experienced winemakers), or you can back sweeten: let the wine continue to ferment to dryness and then add wine conditioner or sugar dissolved in water along with potassium sorbate.

Oaking: If you want to add oak to your wine, you can add it during fermentation or after the wine has been racked for bulk aging. If you are adding oak to your primary, use an oak powder. The oak powder will absorb wine and sink to the bottom of your primary so you get a clean racking. Oak is a very subjective thing; I caution you about adding too much and going too far. A typical volume of oak powder is 4 to 20 grams per gallon (3.8L) of wine.

If you add your oak during bulk aging, you will most likely use oak chips, about ½ ounce (14g) per gallon (3.8L). Take little taste tests to see how the flavor is developing. You don't need to sanitize oak acquired from a reputable source. Just don't use the oak from the tree your neighbor cut down last week!

The Wine Chemist
~ BRUCE ZOECKLEIN ~

If you are inclined to delve into the depths of wine chemistry, meet Bruce Zoecklein. His book Wine Analysis & Production is the essential book on wine chemistry. It takes all the techniques you've read about in this book to a whole new level of fascinating complexity. But, as you'll see here, Bruce also has plenty of straightforward advice for beginners. A California native, Bruce moved to Virginia in the mid-80s. Shortly after arriving, he read a book by a leading wine critic that noted, "Yes, they make wine in Virginia, but one has to ask themselves why." Luckily for Virginia, Bruce stuck around. He headed Virginia Tech's enology grape chemistry group and acted as the Virginia state enologist. Throughout the span of his career, he taught, researched, and provided extensive support for Virginia wineries, which went from a few dozen early in his career to numbering in the hundreds today. He has witnessed and influenced Virginia wineries' transition from mediocre wines to some truly world-class vintages.

Bruce's advice for you is this: remember that everybody starts at square one with knowledge, and that goes for commercial wineries and home winemakers. At first winemaking can seem complex because it is unfamiliar, but the principles are basic. He also advises winemakers to remember the importance of sanitation, to be very attuned to temperatures, and to do your very best to avoid temperature spikes. Bruce believes that our own sensory tools are the best analytical tools we have. Remember to taste your wine frequently; that way you'll note changes in sensory nuances. His other advice is that when you bottle, keep some small portion of your wine in the refrigerator so you can sample it against wine that you have cellared and contrast just how your wine is aging. My favorite of his ideas, "wine makes us lifelong students," certainly rings true for me, and I've a feeling it will for you, too. I cherish receiving his newsletter, Enology Notes. You can add your name to his mailing list by visiting *www.vtwines.info*.

▶ With his extensive experience in the field, winemaking author Bruce Zoecklein played an essential role in developing the winemaking industry in Virginia. He can offer anything from the most expert technical advice to helpful tidbits for the total beginner.

BOTTLING, STORAGE, AND LABELING

Deciding to bottle

When you are absolutely 110 percent certain that your wine is completely finished fermenting, and not a moment sooner, it's time to bottle. You want your wine to be clear and stable.

If your carboy has been finishing in a chilly place, move it to somewhere warm for a few days, just in case the warmth might encourage the yeast to come out of hibernation and continue fermenting. Another sign that the fermentation is complete is that after your last racking, not much more sediment will fall out of the wine. Be patient when it comes to waiting until the time is right for bottling. I've bottled a wine before its time, and it is not a mistake I want to repeat. I'll spare you the details of how much cleanup was involved in the aftermath.

Long before you are ready to bottle, you should have accumulated, removed labels from, and cleaned any recycled bottles, or procured new bottles. The most common size wine bottle holds 750mL (25.4 fl. oz.). Other common sizes are 375mL (12.7 fl. oz.), 500mL (16.9 fl. oz.), and a magnum, which is 1.5L, the equivalent of two bottles of wine.

Before you bottle, calculate the number of bottles you will need. Roughly, you'll get five 750mL (25.4 fl. oz.) bottles for each gallon (3.8L) of wine. It is nice to have a few smaller bottles around in case you cannot completely fill your last bottle.

Bottling

Bottling is lots more fun with friends, and when you're getting everything out to bottle, try to plan to get a few batches done. Also plan to bottle when there will be minimal distractions. You want to get your bottling completed and corks in as quickly as possible to avoid exposing the wine to oxygen or any unwanted contaminants.

Before this point, you should have already made decisions to add any additional sweeteners or preservatives and to rack your wine a final time (if it isn't clear enough to bottle it directly out of the jug or carboy in which it finished fermenting). If you are going to rack a final time, make triple certain that you have washed and sterilized your racking tube, hose, wine filler, corks, corker, and the vessel you are racking into. Also wash, sterilize using a sulfite solution, and drain your bottles. Being organized is key when bottling.

Both your wine and wine bottles should be the same temperature, between 60 and 70°F (15 and 21°C), before you bottle. Have extra towels on hand and do not get distracted; overfilling is a real danger. Dark bottles make it difficult to see fill levels, so working under a good light source is helpful. If you have a helper, that lets things flow smoothly: one person fills and the other corks.

When racking your wine or filling your bottles, use a siphon and move the wine around as gently as possible; you definitely do not want to oxidize your wine at this stage in the process. Fill the bottles to a level about two finger widths below the cork. It takes a bit of practice to get into a groove. Depending on the size of your wine filler tip on your siphon, you might be able to (very bravely) fill the wine almost to the tippy top of the bottle mouth, because when you pull the wine filler back out of the bottle, that brings the wine level back down to optimal.

Fill the bottles to a level about two finger widths below the cork.

Try to bottle with a helper: one person fills and the other corks.

Think ahead a little bit. As with racking your wine, after you have used a little over half of the wine in your carboy, ever so gently tip the jug or carboy onto its side. This way, if there are any unwanted particulates on the bottom, they will settle back down and you won't risk losing your siphon when you get near the bottom, which is all but impossible to get back with minimal volumes. Move the bottom of your siphon to the very corner of the jug or carboy so you get every last drop. When you insert the cork, the surface of the cork should be a hair below level with the bottle mouth—no more than 0.04" (1mm) below.

Immediately mark your bottles as to their contents. My preferred method is to use freezer masking tape and a black permanent marker. After you have corked your wine bottles, leave them standing upright or tipped slightly on their sides for a few days. This gives the corks time to re-expand and make a tight seal. Do a phased tip over where you then turn the cardboard box the bottles are in partially on its side but still propped upright so that the wine covers the cork entirely but does not seep out. A day later, tip the bottles the rest of the way and move them to the cellar. This method is probably overkill, but that's how I do it, and it works for me. Refer to Making Wine from a Kit, page 56, to see photographs and a more simplified presentation of bottling. This is, for sure, one of those parts of winemaking that sounds way more complicated than it actually is.

JUST FOR FUN: BOTTLE TREE

When the flowers fade and the winter winds blow, the beautiful colors of the bottle tree still sing and dance in my garden. I planted my bottle tree to remind me of my winemaking and to enjoy the way the sunlight sparkles through the tree at different times of the day. My bottle tree is also a beacon, reminding me of the beauty that will return as the winter recedes. It recalls one of my favorite Rumi quotes: "Don't think the garden loses its ecstasy in winter. It's quiet, but the roots are down there riotous."

Bottle trees have a good bit of legend and lore associated with them. Essentially, legend gives bottle trees magical properties, and they are purported to keep the home where they are "planted" safe from evil and harm. The cobalt blue bottles are especially attributed with healing qualities, and they "keep the blues away." Bottle trees come in all shapes and sizes, and I think they make beautiful lawn and garden ornaments. And if I get a little bonus good mojo for having one, all the better.

Recycling bottles

Recycled bottles can come from a great number of sources. I need to apologize to my daughter for all those times I teased her that I'd been out looking through neighborhood recycling bins on trash night—in reality, many people have been happy to save their empties for me. If you ask friends to save bottles for you, ask them to rinse the bottles; those mold clouds that waft to the top of messy bottles are icky. Restaurants, social clubs, parties, and special events are great sources of quantities of bottles. In my state, wineries are not allowed to reuse bottles, so wineries can be a great source of bottles, especially after music in the vineyard events or after you participate in winery tour events. Check with restaurants, too. Many diners will leave behind their empties after a BYOB dinner out.

Collect only bottles that are one hundred percent intact; never use anything that has any kind of a crack or a chip. Also make sure that the bottle openings are designed to take a cork. Corking screw cap wine bottles is not a good idea; the openings are often not the perfect size for a cork, nor are the necks on these bottles long enough.

Store your empty bottles in cardboard boxes with the open end of the bottle facing down. This placement helps to prevent dust—or anything else—from entering the bottles.

To remove labels from pre-used bottles, fill the bottle with very warm water. The warmth often releases the adhesive and it's as simple as a steady pull to get the label off. If this works for you, do a happy dance and repeat. If it doesn't work, drop the bottle full of warm water into a large stainless pot, fill the pot with warm water, and let it soak, which makes removal much easier. Be warned: there are those stubborn few labels that require scraping. Having repeated this process over and over for years now, I tease people that one of the ways I judge a wine is by how easily its label peels.

Collect and store used wine bottles for your next vintage.

Corks

As a home winemaker, your choice of closures for your wine is pretty much limited to corks. (Reusing screw caps and reusing corks is not a good idea; it's too risky.) You'll need to decide which cork is right for you. As a general rule, use shorter corks for 375mL (12.7 fl. oz.) bottles and for any wines that will be consumed soon after bottling, and use full size corks for all bottles over 500mL (16.9 fl. oz.). Try to avoid corks that are tapered at the edges; choosing straight corks is your best bet because they give you maximum sealing surface. Also ensure in advance that all of your bottles have standard openings that fit a cork perfectly. Do not reuse wine bottles that have previously had a screw cap.

Corks are still an ideal stopper for wine bottles.

Corks are a classic example of you get what you pay for. The agglomerated corks created from little chunks and bits of cork glued together are very affordable, but definitely not durable. Ideally, you should work with straight up, real, pure corks made from natural cork bark. Synthetic corks that are made from synthetic resins are another choice. And if you ever cut one open, it's fascinating. Manufacturers have made great strides in replicating real cork.

A corker helps to place the cork correctly.

QUICK CORK GUIDE

Cork Size	Use
Short	375mL (12.7 fl. oz.) bottles; wine to be consumed soon after bottling
Full size	500mL (16.9 fl. oz.) and larger bottles; wine to be aged long term

Cork Type	Advantage
Agglomerated	Affordable
Pure	Durable
Synthetic	Durable

Another fun and creative way to personalize your wine is to have customized corks made. They are especially cute if you are creating wines for favors for a wedding, anniversary, holiday gifts, or any other special occasion. Search the web for companies offering this service.

You will want to estimate how many corks you'll need and sterilize a few extras, just in case you have enough wine to fill an extra bottle or two or drop a cork.

You'll have to soften and sterilize your corks before use; there are a number of ways to do so, and I'll share mine. (When I first started beekeeping, an old timer told me, "Ask twelve different beekeepers a question and you will get thirteen different answers." The same goes for cork prep.) I use a floor corker, and it's heavy duty, so I don't need my corks to be all that soft. I simply submerge mine in a water and sulfite bath, move them into a sterilized colander, and cork. If you are using a hand corker, steaming is a great way to soften your corks. Heat water to a boil, remove the water from the heat, drop in the corks, put a lid on the pot, and let the corks steam for a few minutes. Don't steam longer than 3 minutes.

Storing Your Wine

There is such a thing as an optimal space for storing wine, but everyone's facilities are different, so read about the ideal below, then put your creativity to use to see where you can best store your wine.

Wine will be happiest kept between 50 and 60°F (10 and 15°C). Optimally, the temperature will remain fairly constant. The optimal humidity will be between 65 and 75 percent. Low humidity creates the risk of corks drying and shrinking and of allowing your wine to oxidize. If you do have dry conditions, consider a humidifier or placing a bowl of water near your wine storage area. It is handy to have a thermometer somewhere in the storage area. Dark is best, and direct sunlight is a definite no-no. Light degrades wine, and it will affect the flavor and prematurely age it. Wine also likes to be kept very still, so you'll want it far from vibration—no dancing on the cellar floor. Be aware of large appliances nearby, as washing machines, refrigerators, and many devices create vibration when running. Also be aware of heat sources such as stoves and furnaces.

Another very important consideration is preventing any exposure to odors and remembering to not allow fermenting foods or vinegars in the zone. You'll even want to consider what products you use to paint the cellar walls, floor, and shelves.

Store wine on its side. Keeping the cork in constant contact with the wine keeps it moist and helps to prevent shrinking and oxidation. Make sure racks or shelves are very sturdy; as wine accumulates, so does the weight the shelves need to bear. You'll want to organize your cellar as best you can and be sure to clearly mark each bottle as to what it is. You'll also want to organize your layout so that you can get to all of your bottles. You may want to consider keeping a cellar inventory; it's nice to know what you've got, and it'll help you plan for what kind of wine you want to make next. A wine cellar database program can be especially helpful in keeping track of what's aging, what needs drinking, and what will benefit from more time.

Choose a storage area away from light, heat, and vibrations.

BASICS OF IDEAL WINE STORAGE

- 50–60°F (10 and 15°C)
- 65–75 percent humidity
- Dark (no direct sunlight)
- Still (no vibration)
- No other fermentations occurring (i.e., foods)
- Sturdy shelves
- Shelves allowing wine to be stored on its side
- Organization

U.S. FEDERAL WINEMAKING RESTRICTIONS

Federal law allows a two-person household to make up to 200 gallons (757L) of wine or beer per year without a permit as long as it's for personal consumption. Single-person households are limited to 100 gallons (378L) per year. It is also not legal to sell your wine. Check with your local business associations or agriculture extension office for more information about winemaking laws in your area.

A label should reflect your personality and that of the wine.

Kim's paintings suited my labels perfectly.

Labeling wine

Labeling your wines is the ultimate opportunity for creativity—and a mighty good idea if you want to know what's what.

I'll share two of my most "brilliant" failed ideas so that you don't make the same mistakes. Don't just put a simple code (CC for Chilean Chardonnay) in marker on the top of the cork. You'll soon have all sorts of letters and their meanings will blur. Plus, wine may leak out of a cork or mold may grow over the cork, making those letters a real challenge to read. Another idea to skip is simply wrapping different colors of foil around the bottles—as I did, you will surely misplace the list of what the color codes mean.

One method that does work is to use freezer masking tape. Wine cellars can be prone to dust, moisture, and even wine residue (like my wine cellar, from fermentations gone awry), so wait to put official wine labels on your bottles until you plan to use them. Pull the bottle, take the masking tape off, dust it, rinse it if needed (using 60°F [15°C] rinse water), dry it, and then apply a new label.

As you begin to envision what your wine labels will look like, it's inspiring to visit wineries and stores with a nice inventory of wines—all the better if there are finer wines in stock—to gaze upon the myriad labels from around the world. Take note of size, proportion, and where on the bottle your eye most appreciates a label. Notice colors you are attracted to and see what resonates.

The material from which you create your label should be given some consideration. A weatherproof shipping label that needs to be printed on a printer at the office store looks great even if it gets wet. Another consideration is how easily your label will peel if you plan to reuse your bottles for future wines.

There are lots of digital programs and products available that are specifically proportioned for standard sized wine label sizes. Have fun with your label making, and be creative.

Artist Kim Smith painted a variety of artwork for the labels for my wine.

Wine Labels with Flair
~ KIM SMITH ~

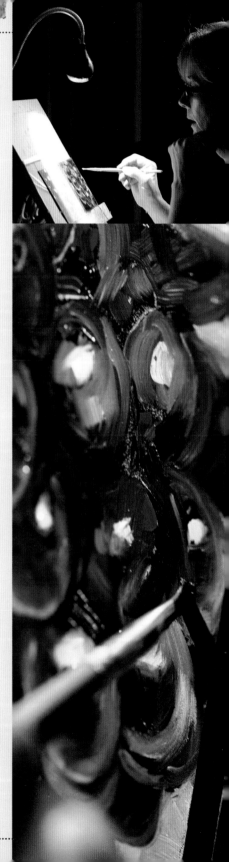

My friend Kim Smith has made a wonderful commitment to creating space in her life for making art. Kim's paintings inspired me to ask for paintings of the fruits my wines are made of. Kim and I worked together to come up with some amazing personalized wine labels; we played with shapes and sizes and finally settled on one label. I often create very small batches of wine and like to bottle them in 375mL (12.7 fl. oz.) bottles, called splits, which are engulfed by a regular size label, so Kim created a smaller sized label for my splits. In the end, the proportion we chose used less label material, which is better for the environment and the budget, and the longer label cropped too much of her beautiful paintings, obscuring and abstracting the fruit. My goal for my wines is to have them be as pure and as true to the fruit as possible, and I love that Kim's gorgeous paintings of the fruit from which my wine is created portray the wines contained within. You can see more of Kim's beautiful paintings at *www.kimmyerssmith.com*.

▶ Of these several versions of wine labels, artist Kim Smith of East Petersburg, Pennsylvania and I chose the one on the right because it showed off the fruit and the smaller label was more environmentally friendly.

Chapter 2
STEP-BY-STEP WINEMAKING

Don't jump in to the winemaking process for the first time with a complex recipe for a dry white wine! In this chapter, you'll begin to learn just how fun and interesting winemaking can be by starting off with a basic winemaking kit. Then, you'll move on to making wine from concentrate. Become comfortable with both of these winemaking methods before you try your hand at the recipes. Plus, meet a talented winemaker who shares some expert tips for checking the status of a fermentation.

MAKING WINE FROM A KIT

Kits are simplicity itself and are the best way to learn. The equipment required is the same equipment you will use in your future winemaking endeavors. The techniques are techniques you will build on when making wine from fruit. With this tutorial, you will learn how to make a French Chardonnay from a kit.

Every kit contains juice, oak, chemicals, very clear instructions, and a list of everything you need to get started. Winexpert, owned by Andres Wines, a large Canadian winery, manufactures a nice selection of wine kits. Recognized for its innovation and dedication to quality, Winexpert is considered to be the leading manufacturer of premium wine kits.

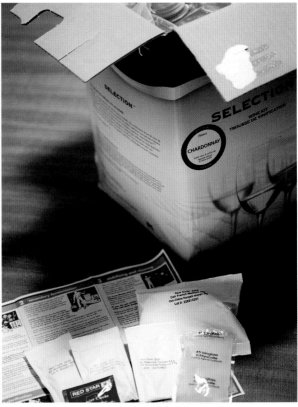

Unpack the kit and gather the materials and ingredients. The kit will include juice, oak, chemicals, instructions, and a materials list.

Before you begin

You'll need to consider a few important items before you start: location, timing, and cleanliness.

Location: The temperature of the area where you leave the wine while it is fermenting should not fluctuate much and should remain somewhere between 65 and 75°F (18 and 25°C). Another important tip is to know that occasionally fermentations get unruly and spew about the surrounding area (know that I've had issues along the way with both primary fermenters and secondary carboys). Choose a spot out of direct sunlight and up on a table so you do not have to disturb what has dropped out of the wine and settled on the bottom when you rack your clearing wine.

Timing: Take a good look at your calendar. Note that the steps need to be done in a certain sequence and in a certain number of days. Ideally, you should plot your starting date based on being available when the following steps need to be carried out. In addition to your own schedule, you may want to consider the earth's as well. Legend, lore, and ancient traditions—even modern-day science—note links between the growing cycles and the cosmos. Within the wine industry, you'll find wine buyers who refuse to taste wines on rainy days and wineries that very carefully schedule dates of tastings for industry experts and buyers based on the lunar calendar. I sync my winemaking activities with the moon phase when I can.

Cleanliness: One of the most important aspects of winemaking from kits, concentrates, or fruits is cleanliness. Sanitize, sanitize, sanitize anything and everything that will come into contact with your wine.

The essential first step to learning is, of course, opening up the kit! Right on top you'll find all the packets and the instructions laid out. Get out your calendar, write the type of wine and the start date, and write the date of the next step.

All the ingredients you'll need will be in your kit.

Always remember to sanitize.

◼ STEP A: PREPARE AND BEGIN FERMENTATION

1

Collect a few gallons (or several liters) of water that is optimal for winemaking as well as a sterilized pot to heat it in. Heat the water; when the water is hot, pour it into the primary vessel.

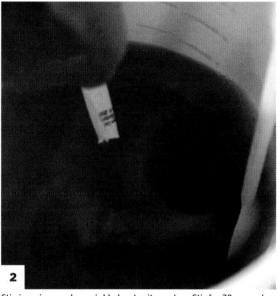

2

Stirring vigorously, sprinkle bentonite on top. Stir for 30 seconds.

3

Add the juice.

4

Add a little warm water to the bag and shake it to make sure you get all the juice.

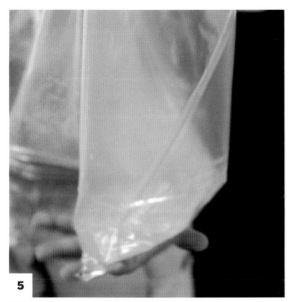

5 Add the remaining liquid in the bag to the fermenter.

6 Top up the fermenter to the 6 gallon (22.7L) mark.

7 Stir well.

8 Sample the liquid with a hydrometer if you have one. However, kits usually fall within the prescribed starting range, so don't worry if you don't have one.

9 Check the specific gravity with the hydrometer.

10 Add the oak, if included.

Check the temperature, and when the juice is between 65 and 75 degrees Fahrenheit (18 and 24 degrees Celsius), open the package of yeast and sprinkle it on the surface. Do not stir.

11

12

Cover your primary, but do not seal the lid tightly, in order to allow the yeast plenty of oxygen. Put an airlock in your bucket and fill the airlock with water.

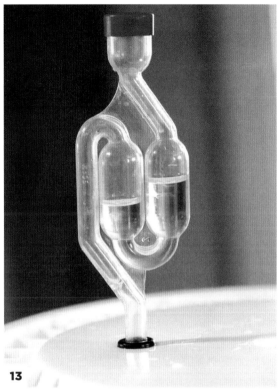

13

Place the kit in a warm spot. Check a day or two later to be sure fermentation has started. You'll notice bubbles and hear it working, and the smell will start to changes.

■ STEP B: TRANSFER TO THE SECONDARY FERMENTER

14

After 5 to 7 days, you'll be ready to transfer your wine from the primary fermenter into the secondary. In the case of this kit, that is a 6-gallon (22.7L) carboy. If you are using a hydrometer, your specific gravity should be 1.010 or less. Sanitize your hydrometer, carboy, siphon, tubing, bung, and airlock before you begin.

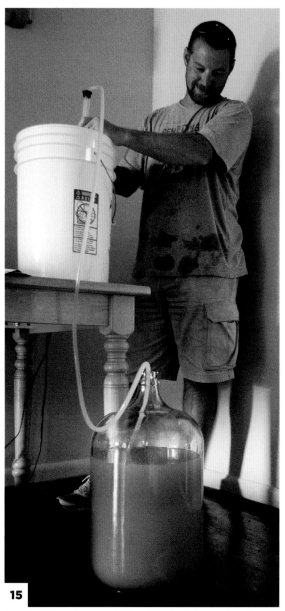

15

To rack, sit the primary up high and the bucket down low, then begin the transfer. The closer in height the fermenters are, the longer it takes to complete the transfer.

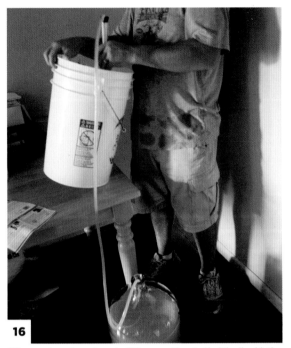

16

After you have transferred a little more than half of the liquid, tip your bucket. Be sure to move the bottom of your siphon closer to the surface while you tip. That way, if sediment gets stirred up, you are not racking it over.

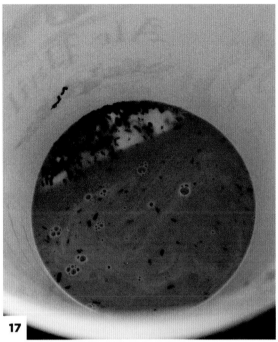

17

As you get near the bottom, move the bottom of your siphon over to a corner of the bucket—still keeping it well above the sediment—and stop before you start sucking up sediment; leave that sludge behind. At this point, you'll have a bit of space at the top of the carboy. Do not top up.

18

Place a bung and water-filled airlock onto the carboy and put it somewhere warm; 65 to 75 degrees Fahrenheit (18 to 24 degrees Celsius) is optimal. Leave it to ferment for 10 more days.

■ STEP C: ADD ADDITIONAL INGREDIENTS

19

After 10 days, or when your hydrometer reading is at the appropriate level according to the instructions with your kit, your wine should be stable. The carboy will have a lot of sediment sitting on the bottom. Dissolve the packets of potassium sorbate (to ensure that your fermentation will not restart) and potassium metabisulfite (to improve your wine's keeping ability) in water.

20

Add the dissolved chemicals to the carboy and stir vigorously.

21

Make sure to stir up all of the sediment on the bottom and get it back into suspension.

22

If you can, use a stirring paddle that attaches to a cordless drill, as shown. A spoon works fine, but you'll need to stir very vigorously.

23

Next, shake your packet of isinglass (to help the wine clarify) and add it.

24

Stir vigorously again.

25

Top up your carboy, and replace the airlock. Good practice is to dump the water out of the airlock, sanitize the bung and airlock, and put fresh water in any time that you rack. Let the wine sit for 8 days.

■ STEP D: RACK INTO A CLEAN CARBOY

26 Rack your wine into a clean carboy. As always, sterilize everything that comes into contact with the wine.

27 Remember to tip the carboy well in advance of the last of the liquid, moving the siphon over to the corner and transferring over only clear liquid.

■ STEP E: BOTTLE THE WINE

Before bottling, rack your wine one final time. (Sometimes you can skip this last racking if there is very little sediment on the bottom.) If you would like to add additional potassium metabisulfite before bottling, this is a good time to do it. Use a very scant amount, and never, never, never overdo it—more is not better. Be sure it is thoroughly mixed in, but be very gentle with your mixing.

28

Make sure your bottles are completely clean, giving them a final rinse with a potassium metabisulfite solution. Be careful to remove any residue if you are using recycled bottles. A new or clean bottle merely needs to be filled with solution and then emptied out.

29

Drain the bottles before lining them up to be filled. Being organized is key to successful bottling.

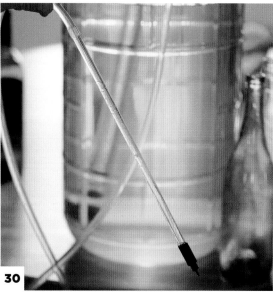

30

Attach the bottle filler to the siphon.

31

When bottling, be sure to add extra liquid for the space taken up by the bottle filler.

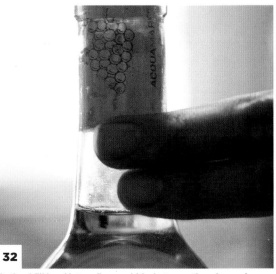

32

Optimal fill level is two finger widths between the wine and the cork.

Group all of your like wine bottles together and fill them in groups. That way, you do not have to readjust the corker multiple times.

33

34

35

Sanitize the corks in a potassium metabisulfite solution before corking.

Cork in groups.

One tip if you are going to use any 375mL (12.7 fl. oz.) bottles is to have a little block of wood or even a paperback book at the ready to put under the bottle. Some corkers cannot reach little bottles without propping them up a bit.

Label your bottles, either with wine labels if your wine storage area is super clean, or with black permanent marker on freezer masking tape. Place the corked bottles into a cardboard box and tip the box just enough so that the corks are in contact with the wine but not enough that the wine could seep out. After about two days in this position, you can safely store them on their sides. If you are using real corks, do store them on their sides to keep the corks moist and fully expanded.

Tah dah! Now that you have successfully made a kit, you are undoubtedly confidently ready to move on to future winemaking endeavors. Making wine from concentrate is the next step.

MAKING WINE FROM CONCENTRATE

Special winemaking concentrates are just that: concentrated fruit juice that you can use to make fruit wine. Many types of concentrates are available to home winemakers. I tend to like a heartier, more robust wine, so I often will add a bit of fruit beyond what the can of concentrate contains. Let's take a look at two examples.

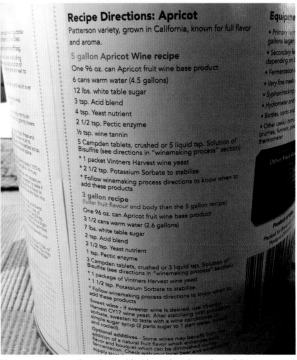

Recipe Directions: Apricot

Patterson variety, grown in California, known for full flavor and aroma.

5 gallon Apricot Wine recipe
One 96 oz. can Apricot fruit wine base product
6 cans warm water (4.5 gallons)
12 lbs. white table sugar
3 tsp. Acid blend
4 tsp. Yeast nutrient
2 1/2 tsp. Pectic enzyme
½ tsp. wine tannin
5 Campden tablets, crushed or 5 liquid tsp. Solution of Bisulfite (see directions in "winemaking process" section)
* 1 packet Vintners Harvest wine yeast
* 2 1/2 tsp. Potassium Sorbate to stabilize
* Follow winemaking process directions to know when to add these products

3 gallon recipe
(fuller fruit flavour and body than the 5 gallon recipe)
One 96 oz. can Apricot fruit wine base product
3 1/2 cans warm water (2.6 gallons)
7 lbs. white table sugar
2 tsp. Acid blend
2 1/2 tsp. Yeast nutrient
1 tsp. Pectic enzyme
3 Campden tablets, crushed or 3 liquid tsp. Solution of Bisulfite (see directions in "winemaking process" section)
* 1 package of Vintners Harvest wine yeast
* 1 1/2 tsp. Potassium Sorbate to stabilize
* Follow winemaking process directions to know when to add these products

Sweet wine - If sweeter wine is desired, use Vintners Harvest CY17 wine yeast. After stabilizing with potassium sorbate, sweeten to taste with a wine conditioner or simple sugar syrup (2 parts sugar to 1 part water, warmed and cooled).

Optional additives - Some wines may benefit from the addition of a natural fruit flavor which enhances the flavor and bouquet which can be diminished during fermentation. Check with your local beer and wine supply store.

Most concentrates for winemaking have handy recipes right on the can.

You can easily add fresh fruit to a concentrate recipe to jazz it up.

PLUM WINE: ADDING FRUIT TO CONCENTRATES

In this example, you'll learn to make a plum wine from concentrate with some fresh plums added to enhance flavor. Often the concentrates will include a recipe within or on the packaging itself that makes either 3 or 5 gallons (11.4 or 18.9L); make only 3 gallons (11.4L) if you want a denser wine with a fuller fruit flavor and body.

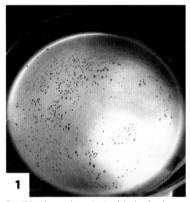

1

For this plum wine, start with the fresh fruit one day ahead. Heat up water.

2

Choose ripe, unbruised fruit.

3

Remove the pits gently.

4

Put the fruit in the primary.

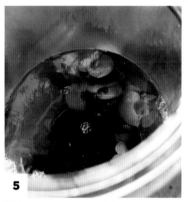

5

Add the warm water and the campden tablet, then partially cover the primary and let it sit at room temperature. The following day, add the concentrate to the the primary and continue by following the label instructions.

■ KIWI WINE: EXPERIMENTING WITH ADDITIONS TO CONCENTRATES

Making wine from a concentrate can be a very simple process, yet, me being me, I carried out a bit of an experiment with the next example. I'd read that using the skin of a kiwi was recommended, and then I'd read that using the skin of a kiwi was not recommended. I had intended to make this batch of kiwi wine straight from the concentrate can, but alas, my curiosity about the "taint factor" of kiwi skins and whether a concentrate augmented with fruit was a vast improvement over a straight concentrate got the better of me. Follow my steps below to carry out the experiment for yourself.

1
Start with a kiwi concentrate, following the concentrate directions on the can to create a 3½-gallon (13.2L) batch using a little less sugar to compensate for the fruit.

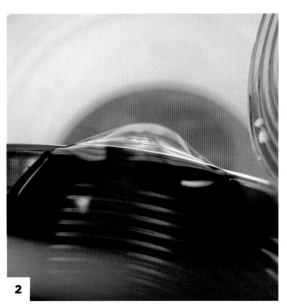

2
Pour the concentrate into the primary fermenter.

3
Add the yeast to start the fermentation.

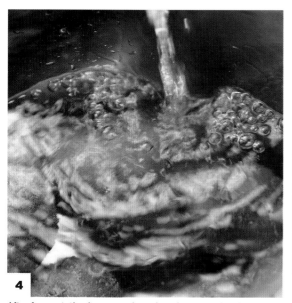

4 After fermentation has started, wash and prepare the kiwis.

5 Leave the skins on for one batch.

6 Peel the kiwi for the other batch.

7 Rack 1 gallon (3.8L) onto the fruit without skins, 1 gallon (3.8L) onto the fruit with skins, 1 gallon (3.8L) into a jug, and the remaining liquid into a ½-gallon (2L) jug, so that you have two primaries: one with skins, and one without.

8

When it is time according to the instructions, rack the wine out of the primary into separate containers.

9

Let the wine ferment. In one glass container is kiwi with skins; in the second container is kiwi without skins. Both were treated with a Campden tablet. Rack the other gallon (3.8L) (the one with no fruit) into a 1 gallon (3.8L) jug and add a small amount of sugar to it to balance out the lack of fruit. Rack the balance into a ½-gallon (2L) jug, and save it to use for topping up when racking the wines off of the fruit. Finish the wines according to concentrate instructions.

When all was said and done with my experiment, all three kiwi wines were delicious. The one made straight from the concentrate was not as interesting as the ones made from fruit. The one with the skins removed was my clear favorite, but the one with the skins on was certainly not objectionably tainted. See if your results are similar.

I've shared this inexact process with you in hopes of showing how you too can be creative in your winemaking. If you are making a batch and curious to know if it will be good with oak or without, divide it and try it both ways. Play. You do have to plan ahead to be certain that you have equipment that will work out nicely with the volumes involved. You also want to remember that high alcohol wines are not very tasty, so do not overdo fruit or sugar additions. You will learn lots by experimenting.

The Art of Fermenting
~ BENJAMIN WEISS ~

With practice, you can go from using winemaking kits to experimenting with and specializing your wine. This is where Benjamin Weiss is now: after years of training and practice, Ben now makes creative mixtures in keeping with his own values and goals. He is a well-studied certified permaculture designer and teacher and an avid wine, mead, and beer maker. I met Ben when I attended a great class he gave on herbal fermentations, meads, and beers.

I asked Ben what advice he might have for beginners to fermentation. Smell your fermentation, he said. If you smell a sour, vinegar-like smell, you know you are in trouble. Also, look at the krausen (the foam and crust atop the liquid in the carboy) and learn to recognize the difference between mold and krausen. He also said that you can gauge a lot by the pace of your fermentation: if it goes very quickly, that is okay; but if it goes very slowly, that can signal a yeast problem. His other advice is to have fun, to start out making inexpensive batches until you gain some experience and confidence, to be meticulous about cleanliness, and to limit the use of chemicals.

▶ Benjamin Weiss of Lancaster, Pennsylvania is a certified permaculturalist, has studied sustainable systems, and teaches classes on fermentations. All his activities keep him busy but ensure that he's always in the know about the best, most ecologically friendly ways to prepare wine.

Chapter 3
DELICIOUS GRAPE, FRUIT & HERB RECIPES

It's time to put your skills to the test with your first recipe. Choose whatever fruit or type of grape you want to try out, and if you can't decide, just choose whatever is in season! In this chapter you'll find 29 diverse recipes, plus ideas for experimenting to make custom wines for your taste. You'll also get a tour of the mass fermentation process (featuring 3,600 pounds [1,632kg] of grapes), and learn about different herbs that can be added to wines.

GENERAL FRUIT WINE RECIPE GUIDELINES

The essential winemaking process for most fruit wines will follow the same sequence of steps. Begin with ripe, sound fruit and prepare it according to the individual recipe guidelines. Place the prepared fruit into the primary fermenter. In a separate container, heat water to just before boiling, then add the warm water and all the other ingredients except the yeast. Take care to completely dissolve the campden tablet before adding it.

Stir the mixture well to dissolve all of the sugar, then loosely cover the must with either a bucket lid or cheesecloth and let it sit for 24 hours in a warm place. Next, add either hydrated yeast or a yeast starter. Allow the fermentation to continue for 5 days, making sure to stir the must two times a day so the ingredients that float to the top do not dry out or begin to mold.

Rack the liquid, without splashing, off the fruit and into a jug or carboy, being careful not to rack over the sediment at the bottom of the primary fermenter. Tightly seal your jug or carboy with a water-filled airlock in a bung and move it to a cooler location, ideally 65°F (18°C).

All of the recipes in this section are designed to yield 1 gallon (3.8L) of wine. If you wish to make a larger batch, simply multiply ingredient quantities by the number of gallons (or liters) you wish to make.

Different fruits are prepared different ways depending on the needs of the recipe.

Standard Fruit Wine Finishing Instructions

Allow your wine to ferment for 3 weeks, then rack it into a clean jug or carboy. Rack again in 2 months, adding one campden tablet per gallon (3.8L). Continue to rack the wine every few months until it is clear and no sediment is visible on the bottom. Your wine is then ready for bottling.

You may want to consider adding a campden tablet again at your last racking to help preserve your wine's color and taste. Be careful not to add too much campden at bottling; beginners have a tendency to overdo it. Some people are sensitive to sulfites, so your decision should be partially based on how quickly you expect to drink your wine. Some fruit wines do not improve much with age and are best consumed within a year of bottling.

Always begin with sound, ripe fruit.

Going Beyond the Recipes

You can successfully experiment in so many ways with your wines, at every stage of the process, with kits and raw recipes—whatever you want to try. There is even real history to support experimentation: there is grappa, an Italian alcohol created from winemaking leftovers, and there are second run wines, made from a second pressing of grapes after normal crushing and pressing has extracted all it could. Let your creativity roam wild. If you create a one-gallon (3.8L) batch and it does not work out for some reason, there is always the possibility of transforming it into spritzers or sangria or using it to enhance your cooking. You can also use wine in marinades and fruit desserts. So go ahead and give it a whirl, and here's hoping you conjure up something lovely. Remember to jot down every pinch of this and dash of that, so if you do want to replicate

The more you experiment, the more amazing batches of wine you'll produce.

what you made, you have a good starting point. Following are just a few of the experimentations I have carried out—let them inspire you.

Mix Fermentations: When I have grapes around, I'll often start a kit combined with a portion of the already fermenting grapes or the pressed skins. I'll also combine those grapes with fruits; reds are lovely with blackberry and blueberry. Sometimes I'll start a batch that turns out to be more than what I need and then combine whatever remains in the primary with another and altogether different batch. I remember making a ginger wine and being like, yowza, this is intense, and keeping one gallon (3.8L) of it just to see how it aged. I combined the rest with peach and eventually part of the ginger peach with raspberry.

Combine Flavors: Another delicious example is if you want to make a thick heavy port or dessert wine and you want to combine things to expand the range of flavors. As I was racking the must off the bananas for banana spice wine, I noted that the bananas still had lots of life left in them. So I decided to take the batch of dried fig and pear I'd just made and put a campden tablet in 8 hours earlier, and combine it with the dregs of the banana spice, and stretch it to a 2-gallon (7.6L) batch of fig with pear and banana by adding more sugar and dates. One snowy Christmas night, I decided that I wanted to create a wine and call it Christmas port. I was racking a blueberry burgundy, and the blueberries were still ok, so I used a grape concentrate and a menagerie of dried fruits. I fortified it with brandy and bottled it in 375mL (12.7 fl. oz.) bottles. Years later, I am still overjoyed when I discover a cork with XP on the top of it, as it seems to get better every year!

Combine flavors in unexpected ways by throwing in additional ingredients like parsley.

Divide It Up: Play by taking your 6-gallon (22.7L) batch and racking it into a five and doing some oaking or flavoring to the other gallon. Divide your six into a 3 gallon (11.4L) and three 1 gallons (3.8L); you end up with four completely different wines this way and learn a lot about flavor combinations in the process.

Add, Add, and Add Some More: Creating new and unusual flavors and the mystery of how they will change over time is one of the greatest aspects of winemaking for me. One of my all-time favorite jazzed-up kits was a blend of three California reds. To this, I added three berries that I had frozen over the summer when they were in season: blueberries, raspberries, and blackberries. Then I added three different kinds of oak: American, French and Hungarian. With those three threes—three kinds of grapes, three kinds of berries, and three kinds of oak—there was no more fitting name than Trinity. It was a wonderful wine; people really enjoyed it. As a beginner winemaker, start out by only mixing two or three flavors and go from there, as it's possible to overdo it.

Use What You Have: I followed recipes exactly for the first few years and fermented lots and lots of different fruits. In time, I developed a sort of Zen winemaking style, having repeated the task enough times to trust myself to start to play. Sometimes I looked at a few recipes as a starting point to approximate how much of this or that would go into a straight batch. Often I didn't even do that; it was more taking all of what I have left of some fruit or dried fruit or using frozen berries to make room in the freezer for some extra venison a friend shared. Or to be given a mega load of pears from a pear tree at a property that friends were rehabbing. Or going to the farmers market and being offered five full cases of raspberries that were fading fast for five bucks and being unable to resist. Winemaking sort of weaves its way into the fabric of your life. If you are open and have the time, the inspiration of abundant fermentation awaits.

REFRESHMENT WITHOUT FERMENTATION

I'd be remiss were I not to mention the importance of responsible consumption and of the value of having a designated driver. A wonderful treat for your designated driver and a great way to hydrate before the first cork is pulled is what we call Angie's Water. It's named after my incredibly brave friend who once ventured half way around the world to serve as nanny for some fascinating people. She came home with this delightful and refreshing way to jazz up water: add a few sprigs of fresh mint and some sliced lemon and cucumber, let it steep, and enjoy. This concoction is tasty almost immediately after being made and continues to grow more delicious as it sits.

USING HERBS AND FLOWERS FOR WINEMAKING

The creative home winemaker (that's you!) can find lots of other fabulous potential ingredients in the plant world. You can make dedicated wines with them, as you will see in the parsley recipe. The main way they are used is to create a tea by steeping them in hot water and then to ferment the strained tea. You can also use them to add complexity and interest to fruit wines. If you would like to add flower petals directly to your must, wait until your fermentation has been going for a few days and is through the most intense part before adding the flowers; petals are so delicate they become decimated when added at the very beginning. Completely remove all the green stuff wherever it lurks—stems, stalks, and leaves. It will make your wine bitter, so be diligent about this. Before you add any herb or flower to a fermentation, be certain to do thorough research into its safety. Nature has her own chemicals and toxins that many people can be sensitive to, and some are outright poison.

In ancient times, there was no other way to preserve things out of season, so they were fermented as a way to preserve and access their properties year round. I'm intrigued with the idea of adding flowers and herbs to create healing tonics. I've had some great successes (a blueberry chamomile that was delicious with a capital D) and some not so great—I'll not make a pure lavender wine again, but I'll most assuredly use a tiny bit here and there. I've been long inspired by Hildegard of Bingen, a nun from the middle ages who was known for, among many other things, her healing powers and use of tinctures and herbs.

My winemaking and gardening are woven together. As I tend to my plants, they inspire me to think of combinations that will complement one another. I love the way rose wine smells, but its taste is lacking something. So this year, I'm determined to make a strawberry rose wine. I've a feeling the two will be lovely together.

When harvesting, pick a sunny morning, after the dew is dry—optimally, a sunny morning amid a few bright brilliant sunny days in a row. Pick the flowers or herbs at peak bloom, not when they are just opening and not as they are waning. Sometimes, it takes a few days or weeks to collect enough, so put the ones you collected in an airtight container and freeze them—very short term—until you have all you need. Use caution about where you harvest. Do not pick any herbs that may have been exposed to pesticides or that are right along the road and have been blasted with car exhaust.

Following is a taste of the herbs and flowers that can become real assets to your wines.

ROSE

The more aromatic the better; rose is lovely in almond wine.

MINT

Mint will add a refreshing taste to watermelon wine.

VIOLET

If you are a patient flower gatherer, try a pure violet wine, or use it to enhance a white, grape, or apple wine.

BEEBALM

Beebalm is nice with raspberry or cranberry wines.

LAVENDER

A pure lavender wine will not go over well, but adding small amounts to other recipes can add another layer of flavor complexity.

Try adding chamomile to a blueberry wine; I had great success when I did! (Recipe on page 96.)

CHAMOMILE

LILAC

Lilac is lovely with a white grape wine.

ROSEMARY

Rosemary will add a whole new dimension to cranberry wine.

BACHELOR'S BUTTON

Bachelor's button combines nicely with pear wine.

ALMOND WINE

MAKES 1 GALLON (3.8L)

¾ lb. (0.3kg) (about 2 c.) raw almonds, blanched, peeled, and cut into small bits

¼ lb. (0.1kg) golden raisins, sliced open

½ lb. (0.23kg) dates, pits removed and chopped

Zest and juice of 2 lemons, strain seeds and pulp

2½ lbs. (1.13kg) sugar

1 tsp. (5mL) yeast nutrient

½ tsp. (2.5mL) yeast energizer

1 campden tablet

¾ gal. (2.8L) water

Yeast (I use EC-1118)

Almond wine is a bit more time consuming but oh so totally worth it. I'm advising that you take the time to peel the almond skin off, as left on it will impart a bitterness that will taint your wine's flavor, scent, and color. This makes a lovely dessert wine.

PREPARATION: Prepare the almonds by plunging them into a pot of boiling water for exactly 60 seconds. The heat will cause the skins to release from the almonds, and you should be able to very easily pull them off. Discard the water and the skins. Chop the almonds into very small bits (if you use a food processor, do not over-process the nuts).

Put the almonds and the lemon zest in the water, and bring it to a boil. Back the heat down until you have a roaring simmer or barely a boil, and leave it for an hour.

METHOD: Put the sliced raisins, dates, and sugar in the primary vessel, then strain the liquid into the vessel. If you are using a glass container, let the liquid cool a bit before pouring it into your primary over top of the ingredients to prevent the glass from cracking. Add the warm liquid a bit at a time to let the glass adjust to the temperature change. Stir until the sugar dissolves.

When the liquid has cooled some, add the campden tablet (dissolved in less than ⅛ c. [30mL] of warm water), lemon juice, and all other winemaking ingredients except yeast. Cover the primary, and allow the must to rest overnight.

Hydrate the yeast in 1.7 fluid ounces (50mL) of warm water, let it sit for 15 minutes, then pitch the hydrated yeast into the must. Ideally, the must and the hydrated yeast should be the same temperature: 70 to 75°F (21 to 24°C) is perfect. Rack after 5 days.

Follow the standard fruit wine finishing instructions (see page 78).

APPLE WINE

MAKES 1 GALLON (3.8L)

8 lbs. (3.63kg) apples (use a mix of varieties)

Juice of 1 lemon, strain seeds and pulp

½ gal. (2L) apple cider

1 lb. (0.45kg) sugar

½ tsp. (2.5mL) pectic enzyme

1 tsp. (5mL) yeast nutrient

½ tsp. (2.5mL) yeast energizer

½ tsp. (2.5mL) acid blend

¼ tsp. (1mL) tannin powder

1 campden tablet

½ gal. (2L) warm water

Spices, such as cloves, ginger, cinnamon (optional)

Yeast (Champagne is nice)

Apple wine is all about the apples. Look for flavorful varieties—Winesap, McIntosh, and Jonathans are great—and combining lots of different varieties of apples is even better. You can even toss in a few crabapples to really help to round out the flavor. Apples are also great combined with other ingredients. I've especially liked apple and pumpkin as well as apple and cranberry combinations. Apple wines are often made from apple juice or apple cider. Look for unpasteurized juice or cider without preservatives.

PREPARATION: Wash the apples. Use only fruit that is firm and ripe and free of rot or damage; remove any bad spots. Then grate or slice the apples. I sliced mine, especially since I was using them with the cider.

METHOD: Put the apples in the primary vessel. To prevent browning, add the lemon juice, campden tablet (dissolved in less than ⅛ c. [30mL] of warm water), and pectic enzyme as soon as you add the apples. Stir in all other ingredients except the yeast. Cover the primary, and allow the must to rest for 24 hours.

After 24 hours, hydrate the yeast in 1.7 fluid ounces (50mL) of warm water, let it sit for 15 minutes, then pitch the hydrated yeast into the must. Ideally, the must and the hydrated yeast should be the same temperature: 70 to 75°F (21 to 24°C) is perfect. Rack after 5 days.

Follow the standard fruit wine finishing instructions (see page 78).

APRICOT WINE

MAKES 1 GALLON (3.8L)

3 lbs. (1.36kg) apricots

2 lbs. (0.9kg) sugar

1 tsp. (5mL) pectic enzyme

1 tsp. (5mL) yeast nutrient

½ tsp. (2.5mL) yeast energizer

1½ tsp. (7.5mL) acid blend

¼ tsp. (1mL) tannin powder

1 campden tablet

¾ gal. (2.8L) warm water

Yeast (Champagne is nice)

Apricot wine is delicious on its own, but apricots also combine well with other fruits. I've had great success with a tart cherry apricot wine. Stone fruits (apricots, plums, peaches, and pluots) can be difficult to clear. I'm presenting two different ways to make wines with stone fruits. Either way, you may end up doing a little more racking than usual until your wine clears.

PREPARATION: Wash the apricots. Use only fruit that is firm and ripe and free of rot or damage; remove any bad spots. Remove the pits, then cut, slice, dice, or mash the fruit—whatever suits your fancy—into your primary.

METHOD 1: After adding the fruit to the primary, stir in all other ingredients except yeast. Cover the primary, and allow the must to rest for 24 hours.

After 24 hours, hydrate the yeast in 1.7 fluid ounces (50mL) of warm water, let it sit for 15 minutes, then pitch the hydrated yeast into the must. Ideally, the must and the hydrated yeast should be the same temperature: 70 to 75°F (21 to 24°C) is perfect. Rack after 3 days.

Follow the standard fruit wine finishing instructions (see page 78).

METHOD 2: After adding the fruit to the primary, add ¾ gallon (2.8L) of warm water and a campden tablet (dissolved in less than ⅛ c. [30mL] of warm water). Let the mixture stand 8 hours, then add pectic enzyme. Stir, and let the must sit for 3 days, making sure to punch down the cap twice a day. Strain, and add all other ingredients. Rack after 5 days.

Follow the standard fruit wine finishing instructions (see page 78).

BANANA SPICE WINE

MAKES 1 GALLON (3.8L)

3 lbs. (1.36kg) bananas (use a combination of perfectly ripe and overripe bananas)

¼ lb. (0.1kg) golden raisins, sliced open

Ginger to taste*

Cloves to taste**

Cinnamon stick (I use 1 stick)

2½ lbs. (1.13kg) sugar

1 tsp. (5mL) yeast nutrient

½ tsp. (2.5mL) yeast energizer

½ tsp. (2.5mL) tannin

2 tsp. (10mL) acid blend

1 campden tablet

¾ gal. (2.8L) warm water

Yeast (I use EC-1118)

My very first batch of banana spice wine was inspired by some bananas that had been neglected and gone way past their prime. Having noted a number of banana wine recipes in various books, I'd long wondered what that would taste like. This wine was one of the greatest surprises ever. It made the most delicious, beautifully colored wine—one of my most raved-about creations ever.

PREPARATION: Wash the bananas, and slice off both ends. Cut the really ripe ones into 1½" (4cm)-chunks and the perfectly ripe ones into ½" to ¾" (1.5 to 2cm)-chunks. Put the bananas and ¾ gallon (2.8L) of water on the stove, and gently heat the mixture over medium heat until it just starts to boil; then, take the heat back down to a simmer for 30 minutes.

METHOD: If you are using a glass primary vessel, let your liquid cool a bit. Then pour it into your primary over top of the sliced raisins and the 2½ pounds (1.13kg) of sugar. Add the warm liquid a bit at a time to let the glass adjust to the temperature change. Stir until the sugar dissolves.

When the liquid has cooled, add a campden tablet (dissolved in less than ⅛ c. [30mL] of warm water), cover, and let it sit overnight. Punch down the cap twice daily; be sure to stir well and submerge the fruit floating on top. Strain off the liquid, and add all of your winemaking chemicals.

Hydrate the yeast in 1.7 fluid ounces (50mL) of warm water, let it sit for 15 minutes, then pitch the hydrated yeast into the must. Ideally, the must and the hydrated yeast should be the same temperature: 70 to 75°F (21 to 24°C) is perfect. I usually wait until the banana liquor has been fermenting for 4 days, then I rack it before adding the ginger and whatever spices I want to use. Rack it again in a week or two, leaving the spices behind.

Follow the standard fruit wine finishing instructions (see page 78).

* I use a very small chunk of ginger that's ½" x ½" (1.5 x 1.5cm), bruised; ginger can be overpowering, so do not overdo it unless you want to maximize the ginger flavor.

** I find cloves to be intense, so I only use 3; more or less is okay depending upon your preference.

BLACKBERRY WINE

MAKES 1 GALLON (3.8L)

4 lbs. (1.8kg) blackberries

2¼ lbs. (1kg) sugar

1 tsp. (5mL) pectic enzyme

1 tsp. (5mL) yeast nutrient

½ tsp. (2.5mL) acid blend

1 campden tablet

¾ gal. (2.8L) warm water

Yeast (I use EC-1118)

Blackberries are a wonderful fruit for winemaking. I enjoy combining them with grape concentrates as they add an amazing dimension. Blackberry season comes and goes quickly. In my area there are a number of pick-your-own places, but because the berries ripen a few at a time, picking appointments need to be made. I've befriended some amazing women over the years whose patches I've picked in, my favorite being a young Amish mother of the cutest, most curious children whose berries are the hugest and most delicious I've ever found. Blackberries also freeze well, and I often save the last of them for winter winemaking adventures. I'm typically not a fan of sweet wines, but with blackberry I do like to back sweeten. It mellows out the tartness of the fruit and makes for a much smoother, more enjoyable wine.

PREPARATION: Wash the blackberries. Blackberries get mushy fast, so don't procrastinate. Resist using berries that are under- or overripe. Be sure to remove any stems or leaves, and gently mash the fruit (taking care not to crush the seeds).

METHOD: Put the berries in the primary vessel. Add ¾ gallon (2.8L) of warm water and the campden tablet (dissolved in less than ⅛ c. [30mL] of warm water), and punch down the cap once a day for 4 days.

Strain the liquid; add the sugar, pectic enzyme, nutrient, and acid, and mix well.

Hydrate the yeast in 1.7 fluid ounces (50mL) of warm water, let it sit for 15 minutes, then pitch the hydrated yeast into the must. Ideally, the must and the hydrated yeast should be the same temperature: 70 to 75°F (21 to 24°C) is perfect. Rack after 5 days.

Follow the standard fruit wine finishing instructions (see page 78), and decide if you want to back sweeten the wine. This wine is best when aged for a year; if you sweeten it, it will be ready sooner.

BLUEBERRY WINE

MAKES 1 GALLON (3.8L)

3 lbs. (1.36kg) blueberries

2½ lbs. (1.13kg) sugar

1 tsp. (5mL) pectic enzyme

1 tsp. (5mL) yeast nutrient

1½ tsp. (7.5mL) acid blend (see note)

¼ tsp. (1mL) tannin powder

1 campden tablet

¾ gal. (2.8L) warm water

Toasted oak chips (optional)

Yeast (Champagne is nice)

I think of blueberries as the closest thing to grapes in the winemaking fruit kingdom. A straight-up blueberry wine is a lovely thing. I've also made some wonderful red wines combining blueberries and grape concentrate, and some very fun mixed-berry variations. Blueberry wine can sometimes be a little challenging due to the presence of sorbic acid in the berries; the fermentation may go much slower than other fruit wines.

PREPARATION: Wash the blueberries. Remove any stems or leaves, and mash the fruit.

METHOD: Add the berries to the primary. Add ¾ gallon (2.8L) of warm water, the campden tablet (dissolved in less than ⅛ c. [30mL] of warm water), pectic enzyme, nutrient, acid, and tannin. Mix well, and let the must rest 8 hours or overnight. Note: After blueberries are picked, their acid content lowers, so just-picked blueberries will need less acid.

Hydrate the yeast in 1.7 fluid ounces (50mL) of warm water, let it sit for 15 minutes, then pitch the hydrated yeast into the must. Ideally, the must and the hydrated yeast should be the same temperature: 70 to 75°F (21 to 24°C) is perfect. Allow the must to ferment for about 5 to 7 days, being sure to punch the cap down daily, then rack.

Follow the standard fruit wine finishing instructions (see page 78), and decide if you want to back sweeten the wine. This wine is best when aged for a year.

CHERRY WINE

MAKES 1 GALLON (3.8L)

6 lbs. (2.7kg) cherries (I love tart cherries, use your favorite)

1½ lbs. (0.7kg) sugar

1 tsp. (5mL) pectic enzyme

1 tsp. (5mL) yeast nutrient

½ tsp. (2.5mL) acid blend

1 campden tablet

¾ gal. (2.8L) warm water

Yeast (I use EC-1118)

Cherry wine can be made from sweet or sour cherries or a combination of the two. It can be a sweet wine or a dry wine. Any way you make it, it is delicious. Removing the pits can be time-consuming, so I tend to just ever so gently break open the cherries and leave the stones. One tip: if you are going to freeze the cherries, you must remove the pits or it will taint the flavor. I have a gorgeous sour cherry tree, but the blasted thing is perilous to harvest from and I can never get enough fruit. Lucky for me, an Amish farmer nearby has gorgeous cherry trees in his orchard and offers pick-your-own. His cherries supplement what I can get from my tree.

PREPARATION: Wash the cherries. Be sure to remove any stems or leaves. Many people take the time to remove the pits from their cherries. I tend to leave the pits, carefully breaking open the cherries without breaking the pits.

METHOD: Add the cherries to the primary. Add ¾ gallon (2.8L) of warm water, the campden tablet (dissolved in less than ⅛ c. [30mL] of warm water), and all other ingredients except yeast. Gently punch down the cap twice daily.

After 24 hours, hydrate the yeast in 1.7 fluid ounces (50mL) of warm water, let it sit for 15 minutes, then pitch the hydrated yeast into the must. Ideally, the must and the hydrated yeast should be the same temperature: 70 to 75°F (21 to 24°C) is perfect. Rack after 5 days.

Follow the standard fruit wine finishing instructions (see page 78), and decide if you want to back sweeten the wine. This wine is best when aged for a year.

CRANBERRY WINE

MAKES 1 GALLON (3.8L)

3 lbs. (1.36kg) fresh cranberries, gently chopped in a food processor

½ lb. (0.23kg) (about 1½ c.) raisins, chopped (I used a 50/50 mix of dark raisins and golden raisins)

Juice of 1 tangerine, strain seeds and pulp

Juice of ½ lemon, strain seeds and pulp

2½ lbs. (1.13kg) sugar

1 tsp. (5mL) pectic enzyme

2 tsp. (10mL) yeast nutrient

½ tsp. (2.5mL) yeast energizer

1 tsp. (5mL) acid blend

1 campden tablet

¾ gal. (2.8L) warm water

FOR THE YEAST STARTER:

Yeast

1.7 fl. oz. (50mL) warm water

Juice of 3 or 4 tangerines, strain seeds and pulp

Cranberry wine is one of the most beautifully colored wines ever. I especially enjoy serving this wine with Thanksgiving dinner. So spot on, it has a bright, refreshing taste and a lovely balance of sweetness to tartness. This wine makes a very fun wine spritzer, too. Cranberry and apple are also a delicious combination.

PREPARATION: Wash the fruit, and remove any underripe or overripe cranberries. Chop the cranberries (I use a food processor; be gentle, don't overdo it).

METHOD: Add the cranberries, chopped raisins, lemon and tangerine juices, and sugar to the primary. Add the pectic enzyme, yeast nutrient and energizer, acid, and the campden tablet (dissolved in less than ⅛ c. [30mL] of warm water). Stir until everything is dissolved and well combined. Let the must rest for at least 8 hours or overnight.

I like to make a yeast starter for this wine. Hydrate the yeast in 1.7 fluid ounces (50mL) of warm water, and let it sit for 15 minutes. Then add the juice of 1 tangerine, wait 45 minutes, add the juice of another tangerine, wait an hour or two, add the juice of another, and so on until you deem it ready or run out of patience. Then pitch the yeast starter into the must. Ideally, the must and the hydrated yeast should be the same temperature: 70 to 75°F (21 to 24°C) is perfect. Allow it to ferment 5 to 7 days. Be sure to punch down the cap twice daily; rack.

Follow the standard fruit wine finishing instructions (see page 78).

CURRANT WINE

MAKES 1 GALLON (3.8L)

2 lbs. (0.9kg) currants

2½ lbs. (1.13kg) sugar

1 tsp. (5mL) pectic enzyme

1 tsp. (5mL) yeast nutrient

1½ tsp. (7.5mL) acid blend

1 campden tablet

¾ gal. (2.8L) warm water

Yeast (Champagne is nice)

Wait to harvest red currants until they are extremely ripe and a deep red color. The fruit is quite tart, even at full ripeness. It makes a light, fresh, tart wine. Red currants and black raspberries also combine well to make a lovely wine.

PREPARATION: Wash the currants. Be sure to remove any stems or leaves, and mash the fruit.

METHOD: Add the currants to the primary. Add ¾ gallon (2.8L) of warm water, the campden tablet (dissolved in less than ⅛ c. [30mL] of warm water), pectic enzyme, nutrient, acid, and tannin. Mix well, and let the must rest 8 hours or overnight.

Hydrate the yeast in 1.7 fluid ounces (50mL) of warm water, let it sit for 15 minutes, then pitch the hydrated yeast into the must. Ideally, the must and the hydrated yeast should be the same temperature: 70 to 75°F (21 to 24°C) is perfect. Allow the must to ferment for about 5 to 7 days, being sure to punch the cap down daily; rack.

Follow the standard fruit wine finishing instructions (see page 78), and decide if you want to back sweeten the wine. This wine is best when aged for a year.

FIG WINE

MAKES 1 GALLON (3.8L)

2½ lbs. (1.13kg) dried figs

¼ lb. (0.1kg) raisins
(I used golden raisins)

¼ lb. (0.1kg) dried pears,
core and seeds removed

2½ lbs. (1.13kg) sugar

1 tsp. (5mL) pectic enzyme

1 tsp. (5mL) yeast nutrient

2 tsp. (10mL) acid blend

¼ tsp. (1mL) tannin

1 campden tablet

¾ gal. (2.8L) warm water

Yeast (Champagne is nice)

Figs are one of my all-time favorite fruits, and they make a brilliant wine. Fresh figs are difficult to come by where I live, so this recipe calls for dried figs. If you want to use fresh figs, increase the amount to 4 pounds (1.8kg).

PREPARATION: Chop the figs, raisins, and pears.

METHOD: Add the fruits to the primary. Add ¾ gallon (2.8L) of warm water, the campden tablet (dissolved in less than ⅛ c. [30mL] of warm water), and all other ingredients except yeast.

Hydrate the yeast in 1.7 fluid ounces (50mL) of warm water, let it sit for 15 minutes, then pitch the hydrated yeast into the must. Ideally, the must and the hydrated yeast should be the same temperature: 70 to 75°F (21 to 24°C) is perfect. Allow the must to ferment for 5 days, being sure to punch the cap down daily, then rack.

Follow the standard fruit wine finishing instructions (see page 78).

WINE MADE FROM GRAPES

The Ideal of Grapes

The grape recipes on the pages that follow differ from the other fruit recipes because grapes are perfectly suited to winemaking. Grapes have natural sugars, acids, tannin, pigments, minerals, vitamins, and even wild yeasts living on their skin. If you are working with optimal fruit, you will be working strictly with grapes—no need to add water or sugar. Following are some generalizations for you to consider so you can tweak the recipes based on your particular situation.

Elements of Grape Wine

BRIX

The first bit of information a winemaker likes to know is what brix (sugar content) the grapes came in at; indeed, grapes often are not harvested until they arrive at the perfect ripeness and sugar content. This information is derived from a refractometer reading made from testing the juice of a blend of a variety of the grapes. Getting that blend can be as simple as picking a few grapes from different places on the vine or from a variety of grapes from different bins or containers squished together in a plastic zip bag to provide an overall representation of your fruit.

If the grapes are overripe, meaning high in brix or sugar content, decide if you are going to dilute the must by adding some water. Wines that are too high in alcohol are not a pleasant experience, but a certain amount of alcohol is needed to help a wine keep. If the sugar or brix is lower than optimal, then winemakers invoke chaptalization of their musts, which means sugar dissolved in water is added to the must to increase the alcohol.

Many variables are considered in optimal harvesting decisions. As a general range of brix, typically white wine is harvested anywhere from 20 to 23; red a little higher at 21 to 23.5 (California grapes are commonly even higher); sweet and dessert wines as high as 26; and sparkling are lowest, starting at 18.

ACID CONTENT

Another key piece of information to have is a sense of the acid content. The general rule is that grapes grown in a warmer climate have lower acidity than grapes grown in cooler climates. As grapes ripen, sugar levels rise and acid levels fall. If the total acidity is too high, wine will be tart and sour. The solution is to dilute the grapes with water. If the total acidity is too low, it creates a wine that is flat and lifeless, quick to oxidize, and that will likely not age well. The solution here is the addition of acid.

HARVEST AMOUNTS

A general rule when making wine from grapes is that you will need 15 pounds (6.8kg) of grapes to make 1 gallon (3.8L) of juice. I find it is sometimes difficult to get 1 gallon (3.8L) of juice out of 15 pounds (6.8kg) of fruit; some grapes are much juicier than others. So my rule is 15 to 20 pounds (6.8 to 9kg), and I'll caution you not to try and pull it off with anything less, as a wine made from pure grape juice is a noble goal.

GRAPE SKIN CONTACT

When making white wine, minimize the contact with the grape skins and the meat of the grape, and carry out fermentations at colder temperatures. When making red wine, go for extended contact with the grape skins, known as cold soaking, and carry out fermentations at warmer temperatures.

OAKING

Go easy with the oak. Consider oaking part of a batch so that you have some unoaked wine to blend in if you need to bring the oak level back into balance.

TERROIR

The terroir is the region of the world where the grapes are grown. I'll share specific information and recipes for several varieties of red and white wine on the coming pages. As a general rule, any grape wine recipe is more or less going to be the same and yet completely different based on terroir. Know that wherever your grapes were rooted, you can make wonderful wines that you'll be proud to share with your friends, family, and especially your winemaking buds.

In ancient times, crushed grapes were put in whatever random vessel could be crafted (cisterns, animal skins, pottery) and the wine made itself. The wine was then put in skins or containers with a reed or a straw as a stopper and sealed with mud. All these years later, we more or less do the same thing. Lucky for us, though, after we crush the grapes, we have abundant known yeast strains to select from and way better containers to ferment and bottle our wine in. I'm reminded of a quote by Clifton Fadiman: "To take wine into your mouth is to savor a droplet of the river of human history."

General Grape Wine Recipe Guidelines

In general, to make 1 gallon (3.8L) of wine, you'll need 15 to 20 pounds (6.8 to 9kg) of grapes, 1 campden tablet, and yeast. In addition, you may also need acid, sugar, pectic enzyme, or yeast nutrient. The recipes that follow give more specific information depending on the type of grape you will be using.

The Grape Wine Process

A few years ago, I was invited to join a group of experienced winemakers to share winemaking with 3,600 pounds (1,632kg) of California grapes. I share the photographic story of this event with you now as a fun introduction to classic grape winemaking.

Our ringleader, Tom Sherlock, had ordered the grapes and designed the recipes. Each step in the process brought us all together, the gatherings made festive with lots of wine tasting, abounding antipasta trays, great music, and lots of laughter. We unloaded, did a quick sort to remove any damaged fruit, then crushed and cold soaked the grapes. The pressing process included the "cutting of the cake," whereby we surrendered and determined that we could squeeze no more juice out. The grape skins were gifted to the compost pile, landing atop the stems from weeks earlier. We aged our wine in oak barrels and at last had a fabulous bottling party. Years later, some of these wonderful bottles are still in my cellar, aging beautifully and saved for special friends, meals, and occasions.

HARVESTING

A batch of grapes fresh-picked from the vineyard.

3,600 pounds of grapes await the start of the winemaking process.

The grapes are sorted off the truck according to variety.

Sorted grapes are labeled and stored until the winemaking process begins.

CRUSHING

The grapes are dumped into the crusher.

The grapes are crushed.

Crushing continues.

The stems are removed . . .

. . . and then composted.

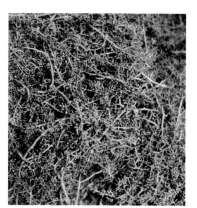

The grape stems really accumulate.

Grape stems are carried off for composting.

The juice that came out of the crusher is moved to the primary fermentation vessel through a funnel.

The plentiful juice keeps flowing.

COLD SOAKING

The crushed grapes are placed in a vessel to begin cold soaking.

Cold soaking continues.

A note identifies the grapes in this cold soak.

Scooping the wine and juice out of the cold soak vessel.

PRESSING

Cold soaked juice and grapes are put into the press.

Bucket after bucket of cold soaked juice and grapes go in.

The press is almost full.

The press is filled to the rim.

The lid is set in place.

Preparing to press.

Adding blocks.

Pressing in progress.

Juice seeps out of the press. . .

. . . and flows into a waiting container.

Tom is about to sample juice coming out of the press.

CUTTING THE CAKE

Removing the press.

All that remains after pressing the grapes are the skins and seeds, compacted into what is called the "cake."

"Cutting the cake" refers to removing the cake.

The cake is composted.

Juice from the pressed grapes is added to the primary fermentation vessel.

All materials and containers are sterilized.

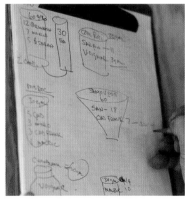

The recipe is finalized.

AGING AND BOTTLING

Some wines age in barrels.

Labels note type and duration.

The bottles are filled.

Corked bottles are ready to store.

OLD VINE ZINFANDEL

MAKES 1 GALLON (3.8L)

20 lbs. (9kg) grapes

1 tsp. (5mL) yeast nutrient

1 tsp. (5mL) acid blend

1 campden tablet

Toasted oak chips

Yeast (I use Pasteur Red)

Old vine zinfandel means that the grapes come from old vines of red zinfandel grapes. Grape vines can live for a very long time, even hundreds of years. One vineyard in California has a zinfandel that dates back to 1865. Older vines are in demand by winemakers because as the vines get older they produce smaller crops leading to more concentrated, intense wines—and one of my all-time favorite reds. When I hear of anyone procuring grapes from California, my first question is, "Can I get any old vine zin?" My very first batch of wine from grapes was from an old vine zinfandel, so I'm pretty nostalgic about it.

PREPARATION: Remove the stems, and crush the grapes.

METHOD: Add the grapes to the primary. Add the campden tablet (dissolved in less than ⅛ c. [30mL] of warm water), yeast nutrient, and acid blend. Punch down the cap, and stir twice daily.

After 24 hours, hydrate the yeast in 1.7 fluid ounces (50mL) of warm water, let it sit for 15 minutes, then pitch the hydrated yeast into the must. Ideally, the must and the hydrated yeast should be the same temperature: 70 to 75°F (21 to 24°C) is perfect.

Allow it to sit for a week, stirring daily to add color, tannins, and flavor to the wine. (Allowing the must to soak somewhere colder will extract less by way of tannins and make a smoother wine.) Then transfer the must to a press and press as much as you possibly can from the grapes—and then press a little harder for good measure. Pour the juice into a carboy, and add oak according to your preferences.

Rack after 3 weeks, then rack every 2 months until the wine is clear and no more yeast deposits form after a 10-day period. Stabilize using a campden tablet dissolved in ¼ c. (50mL) of the wine or using a scant ⅛ tsp. (0.5mL) potassium metabisulfite dissolved in wine; then bottle. Try to wait 1 year before tasting your wine.

CABERNET SAUVIGNON

MAKES 1 GALLON (3.8L)

20 lbs. (9kg) grapes

1 tsp. (5mL) yeast nutrient

1 tsp. (5mL) acid blend

1 campden tablet

Toasted oak chips

Yeast (I use Pasteur Red)

Cabernet sauvignon makes gorgeous, tannic, full-bodied wines. The grape is a cross of cabernet franc and sauvignon blanc. If you can be patient, this is a good wine to age 5 years or more, and when you do, it'll mellow into something amazing.

PREPARATION: Remove the stems, and crush the grapes.

METHOD: Add the grapes to the primary. Add the campden tablet (dissolved in less than ⅛ c. [30mL] of warm water), yeast nutrient, and acid blend. Punch down the cap, and stir twice daily.

After 24 hours hydrate the yeast in 1.7 fluid ounces (50mL) of warm water, let it sit for 15 minutes, then pitch the hydrated yeast into the must. Ideally, the must and the hydrated yeast should be the same temperature: 70 to 75°F (21 to 24°C) is perfect.

Soak for a week, transfer to a press and press completely, then transfer the juice to a carboy and add oak according to your preferences.

Rack after 3 weeks, then rack every 2 months until the wine is clear and no more yeast deposits form after a 10-day period. Stabilize using a campden tablet dissolved in ¼ c. (50mL) of the wine or using a scant ⅛ tsp. (0.5mL) potassium metabisulfite dissolved in wine; then bottle. Try to wait 1 year before tasting your wine.

CONCORD

MAKES 1 GALLON (3.8L)

15 lbs. (6.8kg) Concord grapes

3 c. (710mL) water

½ lb. (0.23kg) of sugar

1 tsp. (5mL) pectic enzyme

1 tsp. (5mL) yeast nutrient

1 campden tablet

Yeast (I use Lalvin 71B-1122)

Concord grapes are also referred to as the fox grape or skunk grape. I'll confess to wrinkling my nose up at the whole notion of making wine from a Concord grape until one Saturday afternoon during a tasting at Coopers Hill Farm. Sandy Witmyer poured a taste, and then a curious thing happened: she added a small bit of simple syrup. I am not much of a sweet wine drinker, but I took a taste of what I expected to be a not-so-great-tasting sweet wine. The most miraculous change had occurred. The whole thing opened up, it smelled better, and when I tasted it, I could taste the grape in a pleasant sort of way. I was astonished. Sandy said, "You have to sweeten Concord a little to bring out its flavor." And I sure enough do.

In addition to sweetening, here are a few other tips. Concord grapes are best picked when they are fully ripe and dark purple. It is better to ferment them at a temperature a little cooler than usual, using a fermenting temperature of 65 to 68°F (18 to 20°C) to minimalize its tendency toward a "foxy" flavor. A general rule is to add one part water to four parts juice and sugar. Concord is not a wine that is typically oaked.

PREPARATION: Remove the stems, and crush the grapes.

METHOD: Add the grapes to the primary. Add all ingredients except yeast. Cover the must, and wait 24 hours. After 24 hours, add hydrated yeast or yeast starter. Stir and punch down the cap at least twice daily for 3 or 4 days. Press, and move the wine into a carboy.

Rack after 3 weeks, then rack every 2 months until the wine is clear and no more yeast deposits form after a 10-day period. Stabilize using a campden tablet dissolved in ¼ c. (50mL) of the wine or using a scant ⅛ tsp. (0.5mL) potassium metabisulfite dissolved in wine. Sweeten if desired to a level that tastes good to you; I highly recommend sweetening this type of wine. If you do sweeten it, you must add potassium sorbate: dissolve ½ tsp. (2.5mL) potassium sorbate along with your campden tablet or sulfite. Bottle and age two years before tasting.

SEYVAL BLANC

MAKES 1 GALLON (3.8L)

20 lbs. (9kg) grapes

1 tsp. (5mL) yeast nutrient

½ tsp. (2.5mL) acid blend

¾ lb. (0.34kg) sugar dissolved in 2 c. (470mL) warm water

1 campden tablet

Toasted oak chips

Yeast (I use Lalvin K1-V1116)

Seyval blanc is a hybrid that is well suited to cool climates, and I'm ever so thankful that it grows in the vineyard at Coopers Hill Farm. My goal with this wine was to create a crisp, dry, lightly oaked, aromatic wine with a certain sense of terroir and minerality.

I wanted to carry out this fermentation at very cool temperatures so I could retain the intrinsic qualities of the grape, which meant yeast selection was important. Cote des Blancs and Premier Cuvee would have been fine choices, but I went with K1-V1116 because it overcomes wild yeasts, gets off to a quick start, and carries out a constant and complete fermentation at temperatures as low as 50°F (10°C). K1-V1116 is also known for making wines that express the freshness of the grape, retaining natural fresh fruit aromas far longer than many other yeast strains.

PREPARATION: Remove the stems, then crush and press the grapes immediately to minimalize skin contact.

METHOD: Add the grapes to the primary. Add the campden tablet (dissolved in less than ⅛ c. [30mL] of warm water), yeast nutrient, acid blend, and sugar dissolved in warm water.

After 24 hours, hydrate the yeast in 1.7 fluid ounces (50mL) of warm water, let it sit for 15 minutes, then pitch the hydrated yeast into the must. Ideally, the must and the hydrated yeast should be the same temperature: 70 to 75°F (21 to 24°C) is perfect.

Carry out fermentation, and continue to keep the wine sitting somewhere very cool; 55°F (13°C) is ideal. This is when I add oak (I'll leave the amount up to your preferences).

It is very important that you rack this wine as soon as fermentation ceases, as it can pick up off flavors if it sits. Rack every month until the wine is clear and no more yeast deposits form after a 10-day period. Stabilize using a campden tablet dissolved in ¼ c. (50mL) of the wine or using a scant ⅛ tsp. (0.5mL) potassium metabisulfite dissolved in wine; then bottle. Try to wait 6 months before tasting your wine.

VIDAL BLANC

MAKES 1 GALLON (3.8L)

20 lbs. (9kg) grapes

1 tsp. (5mL) yeast nutrient

1 campden tablet

Toasted oak chips

Yeast (I use K1-V1116)

Vidal blanc is another cold, hardy grape that is also grown at Coopers Hill Farm. Vidal blanc is a versatile grape that was originally developed for use in cognac. Thick-skinned and very acidic, it is produced to make both dry and sweet wines. Vidal blanc makes a lovely, very fruity, aromatic wine. Because it is very winter hardy, it is popular in parts north and Canada for use in ice wine.

PREPARATION: Remove the stems, then crush and press the grapes immediately to minimalize skin contact.

METHOD: Add the grapes to the primary. Add the campden tablet (dissolved in less than ⅛ c. [30mL] of warm water) and yeast nutrient.

After 24 hours, hydrate the yeast in 1.7 fluid ounces (50mL) of warm water, let it sit for 15 minutes, then pitch the hydrated yeast into the must. Ideally, the must and the hydrated yeast should be the same temperature: 70 to 75°F (21 to 24°C) is perfect.

Rack as soon as fermentation has ceased. This is where I add oak (I'll leave the amount up to your preferences). Remember to ferment and store the wine at a cool temperature: 55°F (13°C) is ideal.

Rack every month until the wine is clear and no more yeast deposits form after a 10-day period. Stabilize using a campden tablet dissolved in ¼ c. (50mL) of the wine or using a scant ⅛ tsp. (0.5mL) potassium metabisulfite dissolved in wine; then bottle. Bottle this wine young, and consume it young.

RIESLING

MAKES 1 GALLON (3.8L)

20 lbs. (9kg) grapes

1 tsp. (5mL) yeast nutrient

1 campden tablet

Yeast (I use K1-V1116)

Riesling is a very popular and very versatile grape. Again, I can find it just up the hill from me at Coopers Hill Farm. When I got a call that some were still hanging on the vine and did I want to come and pick, you know I said yes. I'm a big fan of oak, but in researching, I discovered that this wine is seldom oaked.

PREPARATION: Remove the stems, then crush and press grapes immediately to minimalize skin contact.

METHOD: Add the grapes to the primary. Add the campden tablet (dissolved in less than ⅛ c. [30mL] of warm water) and yeast nutrient.

After 24 hours, hydrate the yeast in 1.7 fluid ounces (50mL) of warm water, let it sit for 15 minutes, then pitch the hydrated yeast into the must. Ideally, the must and the hydrated yeast should be the same temperature: 70 to 75°F (21 to 24°C) is perfect.

Rack as soon as fermentation has ceased. Ferment and store at a cool temperature: 55°F (13°C) is ideal.

Rack every month until the wine is clear and no more yeast deposits form after a 10-day period. Stabilize using a campden tablet dissolved in ¼ c. (50mL) of the wine or using a scant ⅛ tsp. (0.5mL) potassium metabisulfite dissolved in wine; then bottle. Rieslings, especially sweet ones, are sometimes suitable for extended aging. I'd advise drinking this one after 3–6 months and intermittently thereafter so you can keep track of how it is aging. You do not want to wait a long time and risk it going past its prime.

California Grape Run

This year our group of winemakers was being pulled in every direction and the grapes we wanted came a week early, when the truck and trailer were needed to do a big festival. We decided to just let it go—but I could not let it go! So I began a frantic web and phone search for California grapes on the East Coast. Time was not my friend; I was late in the game and I knew it.

But I managed to locate some grapes, and off on an adventure I went. A massive produce hub awaited me, my little Subaru dwarfed by tractor-trailers. A rather daunting gated entry greeted me upon arrival, and finding my way to just the right bay was a whole other adventure. Finally, I found what I sought, and off I went, Subaru tires showing the strain under a load of as many cases of grapes as I could cram in my vehicle along with two 13-gallon (49.2L) carboys I simply could not resist purchasing.

It was a charmed journey for sure. En route home, I stopped at a beer and wine supply shop I don't often get to due to its distance from my house. I was after a particular yeast, but lo and behold, as I entered, the first thing my eyes landed upon was the cutest little press I ever did see. Don't ask me to tell you of the magic I performed to fit that in the car, but fit it did. Here are just a few photographs from my journey to score old vine zinfandel and cabernet sauvignon grapes.

S&S
Winegrapes
at
Sudano's
Produce

MULBERRY WINE

MAKES 1 GALLON (3.8L)

3½ lbs. (1.6kg) mulberries

1½ lbs. (0.7kg) sugar

1 tsp. (5mL) pectic enzyme

1 tsp. (5mL) yeast nutrient

½ tsp. (2.5mL) acid blend

1 campden tablet

¾ gal. (2.8L) warm water

Yeast (I use EC-1118)

I'll be honest here: mulberry wine is not my favorite. However, the price is certainly right. Mulberry trees abound and with age grow massive and produce lots of fruit. This wine is a great candidate for adding other ingredients to jazz it up. I encourage you to be creative.

PREPARATION: Wash the fruit. Mulberries get mushy fast, so don't procrastinate. Resist using berries that are underripe or overripe. Remove any stems or leaves, and gently mash the fruit.

METHOD: Add the fruit to the primary. Add ¾ gallon (2.8L) of warm water, the campden tablet (dissolved in less than ⅛ c. [30mL] of warm water), and all other ingredients except yeast. Be sure to punch down the cap twice daily.

After 24 hours, hydrate the yeast in 1.7 fluid ounces (50mL) of warm water, let it sit for 15 minutes, then pitch the hydrated yeast into the must. Ideally, the must and the hydrated yeast should be the same temperature: 70 to 75°F (21 to 24°C) is perfect. Rack after 5 days.

Follow the standard fruit wine finishing instructions (see page 78), and decide if you want to back sweeten the wine. This wine is best when aged for a year.

PARSLEY WINE

MAKES 1 GALLON (3.8L)

1 lb. (0.45kg) fresh parsley
(I like the Italian flat leaf, but use
what you have or a mixture)

Juice of 2 oranges, strain seeds
and pulp (I use tangelos or
whatever nice oranges I can find)

Juice of 2 lemons, strain
seeds and pulp

2½ lbs. (1.13kg) sugar

½ tsp. (2.5mL) pectic enzyme

1 tsp. (5mL) yeast nutrient

½ tsp. (2.5mL) yeast energizer

4 tsp. (20mL) acid blend

½ tsp. (2.5mL) tannin

1 campden tablet

¾ gal. (2.8L) warm water

Yeast (I use 71B-1122)

Parsley wine was another one of those incredibly pleasant surprises. I was not at all sure why I was even attempting this wine the first time around. Something about the idea of a parsley wine just intrigued me, and I sure am glad it did.

PREPARATION: Wash the parsley. Tear the parsley apart a bit; you can use stems, leaves, and all. Combine the water, orange and lemon zests, and parsley in a pot on the stove and bring it to a boil; simmer for 20 minutes.

METHOD: Strain the simmered mixture, then pour the liquid onto the sugar in the primary; stir well until the sugar is fully dissolved. When the liquid is lukewarm, below 75°F (24°C), add the orange and lemon juices and all of the other ingredients except the yeast.

Hydrate the yeast in 1.7 fluid ounces (50mL) of warm water, let it sit for 15 minutes, then pitch the hydrated yeast into the must. Ideally, the must and the hydrated yeast should be the same temperature: 70 to 75°F (21 to 24°C) is perfect. Rack after 4 or 5 days.

Follow the standard fruit wine finishing instructions (see page 78).

PAW PAW WINE

Way down yonder in the paw paw patch awaits a lovely wine. I'll confess: it's not fun to make, as paw paws are a most unusual fruit and the peeling and seed removal is more of a chore with this fruit than any other I can think of. The wine, though, is delicious. If you have access to paw paws and time on your hands, making paw paw wine is worth the effort for certain.

PREPARATION: Wash and peel the fruit, and remove the seeds. This is a bit of a daunting task. Keep a second small vessel with a bit of water and drop seeds into it as you remove them. Try to wash the fruit that clings to the seeds into the water so you get every bit of fruit you can for fermenting. Mash the fruit.

MAKES 1 GALLON (3.8L)

3 lbs. (1.36kg) paw paws

2¼ lbs. (1kg) sugar

1 tsp. (5mL) pectic enzyme

1 tsp. (5mL) yeast nutrient

1½ tsp. (7.5mL) acid blend

½ tsp. (2.5mL) tannin powder

1 campden tablet

¾ gal. (2.8L) warm water

Yeast (Champagne is nice)

METHOD: Add the fruit to the primary. Add ¾ gallon (2.8L) of warm water, the campden tablet (dissolved in less than ⅛ c. [30mL] of warm water), pectic enzyme, nutrient, acid, and tannin. Mix well, and let the must sit 8 hours or overnight.

Hydrate the yeast in 1.7 fluid ounces (50mL) of warm water, let it sit for 15 minutes, then pitch the hydrated yeast into the must. Ideally, the must and the hydrated yeast should be the same temperature: 70 to 75°F (21 to 24°C) is perfect. Allow it to ferment for about a week, then rack.

Follow the standard fruit wine finishing instructions (see page 78). This wine may need to be racked multiple times to clear. It is best when aged for a year.

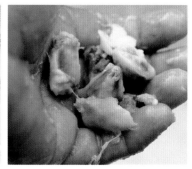

PEACH WINE

MAKES 1 GALLON (3.8L)

3 lbs. (1.36kg) peaches

2 lbs. (0.9kg) sugar

1 tsp. (5mL) pectic enzyme

1 tsp. (5mL) yeast nutrient

½ tsp. (2.5mL) yeast energizer

1½ tsp. (7.5mL) acid blend

¼ tsp. (1mL) tannin powder

1 campden tablet

¾ gal. (2.8L) warm water

Yeast (Champagne is nice)

Peach wine is a little like strawberry wine for me—it's oh so difficult to resist eating those ripe, juicy, succulent, gorgeous fruits I'm supposed to be fermenting, and it's such a reminder of summer when sipped. I've also made and really enjoyed ginger peach wine and raspberry ginger peach wine. Stone fruits (apricots, plums, peaches, and pluots) can be difficult to clear. See the Apricot Wine recipe, page 90, for a second method for making wine from stone fruits.

PREPARATION: Wash the peaches. Use only fruit that is firm and ripe and free of rot or damage; remove any bad spots. Remove the pits, or leave just a few if you like the nutty, almost almond-like flavor they impart. Cut the fruit.

METHOD: Add the fruit to the primary. Stir in all other ingredients except the yeast. Cover the primary, and let the must rest for 24 hours.

After 24 hours, hydrate the yeast in 1.7 fluid ounces (50mL) of warm water, let it sit for 15 minutes, then pitch the hydrated yeast into the must. Ideally, the must and the hydrated yeast should be the same temperature: 70 to 75°F (21 to 24°C) is perfect. Rack after 3 days.

Follow the standard fruit wine finishing instructions (see page 78).

PEAR WINE

MAKES 1 GALLON (3.8L)

6 lbs. (2.7kg) pears (ripe, sweet, and juicy), chopped with cores removed

½ lb. (0.23kg) (about 1½ c.) golden raisins, chopped

Juice of ½ lemon, strain seeds and pulp

3 lbs. (1.36kg) sugar

½ tsp. (2.5mL) pectic enzyme

1 tsp. (5mL) yeast nutrient

½ tsp. (2.5mL) yeast energizer

1 tsp. (5mL) acid blend

1 campden tablet

¾ gal. (2.8L) warm water

Yeast (I use 71B-1127)

Pears come in many shapes and sizes, each variety with its own particular flavor characteristics. However, even with all that variety to experiment with, I've yet to create a pear wine that I adored. That said, I continue to make pear wines in hopes of finally creating that elusive delicious pear wine that I know awaits conjuring. I've decided that I will add some dried pears to my next batch of pear wine in hopes that they will deepen the flavor.

PREPARATION: Wash the pears and remove the core and any bad spots. Chop the pears.

METHOD: Add the pears to the primary, then add the chopped raisins, lemon juice, and sugar. Add the pectic enzyme, yeast nutrient and energizer, acid, and the campden tablet (dissolved in less than ⅛ c. [30mL] of warm water). Stir until everything is dissolved and well combined. Let the must rest for at least 8 hours or overnight.

Hydrate the yeast in 1.7 fluid ounces (50mL) of warm water, let it sit for 15 minutes, then pitch the hydrated yeast into the must. Ideally, the must and the hydrated yeast should be the same temperature: 70 to 75°F (21 to 24°C) is perfect. Rack after 5 days, making sure to punch down the cap twice daily.

Follow the standard fruit wine finishing instructions (see page 78).

PLUM WINE

MAKES 1 GALLON (3.8L)

4 lbs. (1.8kg) plums

2 lbs. (0.9kg) sugar

1 tsp. (5mL) pectic enzyme

1 tsp. (5mL) yeast nutrient

½ tsp. (2.5mL) yeast energizer

1½ tsp. (7.5mL) acid blend

¼ tsp. (1mL) tannin powder

1 campden tablet

¾ gal. (2.8L) warm water

Yeast (Champagne is nice)

Plum wine can be flat out amazing. I like to use a blend of as many different varieties of plums as I can find: yellow, red, magenta, and deep dark purple. Each variety of plum has its own unique colored flesh—some sweet, some tart, some sweet and tart all rolled into one. All are lovely, but when combined, they make some magical elixirs. Stone fruits (apricots, plums, peaches, and pluots) can be difficult to clear. See the Apricot Wine recipe, page 90, for a second method to make wine from stone fruits.

PREPARATION: Wash the plums. Use only fruit that is firm and ripe and free of rot or damage; remove any bad spots. Remove the pits, and cut the fruit.

METHOD: Add the plums to the primary. Stir in all other ingredients except the yeast. Cover the primary and let the must rest after 24 hours.

After 24 hours, hydrate the yeast in 1.7 fluid ounces (50mL) of warm water, let it sit for 15 minutes, then pitch the hydrated yeast into the must. Ideally, the must and the hydrated yeast should be the same temperature: 70 to 75°F (21 to 24°C) is perfect. Rack after 3 days.

Follow the standard fruit wine finishing instructions (see page 78).

PLUOT WINE

Pluots are a beautiful hybrid of plums and apricots—more plum than apricot and very sweet. I'm fascinated by plant genetics. These fruits were created by a fruit breeder in California who used a fruit called a plumcot, which was a 50/50 mix of plum and apricot developed in the late 10th century by Luther Burbank, a man who literally created hundreds of varieties of nuts, fruits, and flowers.

PREPARATION: Wash the pluots. Use only fruit that is firm and ripe and free of rot or damage; remove any bad spots. Remove the pits, and cut the fruit.

METHOD: Add the pluots to the primary. Stir in all other ingredients except the yeast. Cover the primary, and allow the must to rest for 24 hours.

After 24 hours, hydrate the yeast in 1.7 fluid ounces (50mL) of warm water, let it sit for 15 minutes, then pitch the hydrated yeast into the must. Ideally, the must and the hydrated yeast should be the same temperature: 70 to 75°F (21 to 24°C) is perfect. Rack after 3 days.

Follow the standard fruit wine finishing instructions (see page 78).

MAKES 1 GALLON (3.8L)

3 lbs. (1.36kg) pluots

2¼ lbs. (1kg) sugar

1 tsp. (5mL) pectic enzyme

1 tsp. (5mL) yeast nutrient

½ tsp. (2.5mL) yeast energizer

1½ tsp. (7.5mL) acid blend

¼ tsp. (1mL) tannin powder

1 campden tablet

¾ gal. (2.8L) warm water

Yeast (Champagne is nice)

PUMPKIN WINE

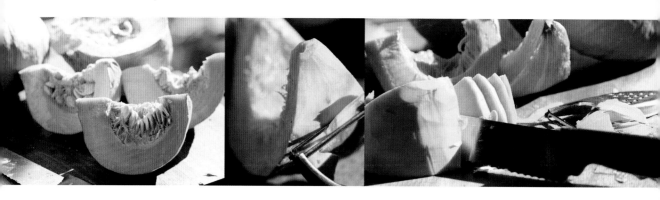

MAKES 1 GALLON (3.8L)

3 lbs. (1.36kg) pumpkin meat, chopped or grated into small pieces with seeds removed (I used a kobocha squash, but any sweet pumpkin will do)

2 apples, chopped and core removed (I used a granny smith and a honeycrisp)

½ lb. (0.23kg) (about 1½ c.) raisins, chopped (I used a 50/50 blend of dark raisins and golden raisins)

Juice of ½ lemon, strain seeds and pulp

2½ lbs. (1.13kg) sugar

½ tsp. (2.5mL) pectic enzyme

1 tsp. (5mL) yeast nutrient

½ tsp. (2.5mL) yeast energizer

1½ tsp. (7.5mL) acid blend

1 campden tablet

¾ gal. (2.8L) warm water

Spices (ginger, cinnamon, and cloves would all be lovely)

Yeast (I use 71B-1127)

Any number of varieties of pumpkins is available for your winemaking pleasure. They are a bit unruly to work with, requiring a very sharp knife and patience, but oh so worth it. Be careful not to overdo it with adding spices.

PREPARATION: Prepare the squash and apples by cleaning and chopping.

METHOD: Add the squash and apples to the primary. Add the chopped raisins, lemon juice, and sugar. Add the pectic enzyme, yeast nutrient and energizer, acid, and the campden tablet (dissolved in less than ⅛ c. [30mL] of warm water). Stir until everything is dissolved and well combined. Let the must sit for at least 8 hours or overnight.

Hydrate the yeast in 1.7 fluid ounces (50mL) of warm water, let it sit for 15 minutes, then pitch the hydrated yeast into the must. Ideally, the must and the hydrated yeast should be the same temperature: 70 to 75°F (21 to 24°C) is perfect. Allow it to ferment 5 days, making sure to punch down the cap twice daily, and rack.

Follow the standard fruit wine finishing instructions (see page 78).

RASPBERRY WINE

MAKES 1 GALLON (3.8L)

3 lbs. (1.36kg) raspberries (red or black, or a combination of both)

2¼ lbs. (1kg) sugar

1 tsp. (5mL) pectic enzyme

1 tsp. (5mL) yeast nutrient

½ tsp. (2.5mL) acid blend

1 campden tablet

¾ gal. (2.8L) warm water

Yeast (I use EC-1118)

Raspberry wine has a magnificent flavor. I especially like the results when I mix different kinds of raspberries together. The flavor is fairly intense, and this is another wine that I advise back sweetening a bit to mellow it out.

PREPARATION: Wash the fruit. Raspberries get mushy fast, so don't procrastinate. Resist using berries that are underripe or overripe. Remove any stems or leaves, and mash the fruit, taking care not to crush the seeds.

METHOD: Add the berries to the primary. Add ¾ gallon (2.8L) of warm water and the campden tablet (dissolved in less than ⅛ c. [30mL] of warm water). Punch down the cap once a day for 4 days. Strain the liquid. Add the sugar, pectic enzyme, nutrient, and acid. Mix well.

Hydrate the yeast in 1.7 fluid ounces (50mL) of warm water, let it sit for 15 minutes, then pitch the hydrated yeast into the must. Ideally, the must and the hydrated yeast should be the same temperature: 70 to 75°F (21 to 24°C) is perfect. Allow it to ferment for about 5 to 7 days, then rack.

Follow the standard fruit wine finishing instructions (see page 78), and decide if you want to back sweeten the wine. This wine is best when aged for a year.

STRAWBERRY WINE

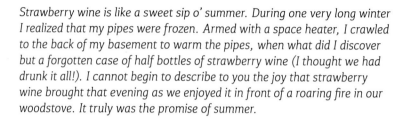

MAKES 1 GALLON (3.8L)

3 lbs. (1.36kg) strawberries

2½ lbs. (1.13kg) sugar

1 tsp. (5mL) pectic enzyme

1 tsp. (5mL) yeast nutrient

½ tsp. (2.5mL) yeast energizer

2 tsp. (10mL) acid blend

¼ tsp. (1mL) tannin powder

1 campden tablet

¾ gal. (2.8L) warm water

Yeast (Champagne is nice)

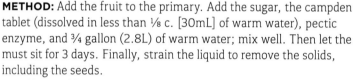

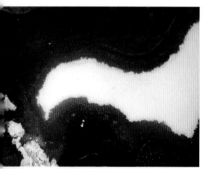

Strawberry wine is like a sweet sip o' summer. During one very long winter I realized that my pipes were frozen. Armed with a space heater, I crawled to the back of my basement to warm the pipes, when what did I discover but a forgotten case of half bottles of strawberry wine (I thought we had drunk it all!). I cannot begin to describe to you the joy that strawberry wine brought that evening as we enjoyed it in front of a roaring fire in our woodstove. It truly was the promise of summer.

PREPARATION: Mash the fruit. I've heard it said that the seeds in the strawberries, miniscule though they are, taint the flavor of the strawberry wine. I've made it with and without the seeds, and I'm still not sure that the "taint" is all that much of a concern. If you decide you want to avoid the risk of seeds tainting your wine's flavor, the solution is simple enough: add a straining step as described below.

METHOD: Add the fruit to the primary. Add the sugar, the campden tablet (dissolved in less than ⅛ c. [30mL] of warm water), pectic enzyme, and ¾ gallon (2.8L) of warm water; mix well. Then let the must sit for 3 days. Finally, strain the liquid to remove the solids, including the seeds.

Next, add nutrient, energizer, acid, and tannin. Hydrate the yeast in 1.7 fluid ounces (50mL) of warm water, let it sit for 15 minutes, then pitch the hydrated yeast into the must. Ideally, the must and the hydrated yeast should be the same temperature: 70 to 75°F (21 to 24°C) is perfect. Allow it to ferment for about a week, then rack.

Follow the standard fruit wine finishing instructions (see page 78). Back sweeten before bottling and age for a year.

WATERMELON WINE

MAKES 1 GALLON (3.8L)

3 lbs. (1.36kg) melon (use the center of the melon and remove the seeds)

2 lbs. (0.9kg) sugar

½ tsp. (2.5mL) pectic enzyme

1 tsp. (5mL) yeast nutrient

2 tsp. (10mL) acid blend

1 campden tablet

Water to make a gallon (3.8L) (It's difficult to predict how much liquid you'll get)

Yeast (I use EC-1118)

Watermelon wine is quite an unusual wine. The first time I made it, we had been at an all-day lacrosse tournament and one of the other moms was about to throw away two big plastic zipper bags of cut-up watermelon and grapes. Of course, I swooped in and said, "Oh, I'll ferment those," and, miraculously, the wine turned out great.

The best and most flavorful melons seem to be those old varieties that have the seeds, and yes, it is a pain to remove those seeds. I mixed some with seeds and some without seeds; their presence doesn't seem to matter. However, you want to work with only the sweet part of the melon. That fruit out near the rind is not going to do your wine any favors. I'll caution you that watermelon is tricky stuff to work with, and it can get nasty quick.

PREPARATION: Wash the melon. Cut the melon into cubes.

METHOD: Add the melon to the primary. Add the campden tablet (dissolved in less than ⅛ c. [30mL] of warm water) and all other ingredients except the yeast. Be sure to gently punch down the cap twice daily. After 24 hours, hydrate the yeast in 1.7 fluid ounces (50mL) of warm water, let it sit for 15 minutes, then pitch the hydrated yeast into the must. Ideally, the must and the hydrated yeast should be the same temperature: 70 to 75°F (21 to 24°C) is perfect. Allow it to ferment for about 3 days, then rack.

Follow the standard fruit wine finishing instructions (see page 78), and decide if you want to back sweeten the wine. This wine is best when aged for a year.

SANGRIA

⅛ lb. (0.05kg) (about ¼ c.) sugar

½ c. (120mL) water

2 stalks rhubarb, diced

1 orange, sliced thinly

1 lemon, sliced thinly

2 or 3 heaping handfuls fresh, ripe red strawberries, sliced

Handful mulberries

1 or 2 shots spiced rum (optional)

1 bottle (750mL [25.4 fl. oz.]) chardonnay

1 can (111.15 fl. oz.) sparkling blood orange San Pellegrino

½ c. (120mL) orange peach mango juice (or orange juice or blood orange juice)

Few sprigs of lemon verbena

The perfect summer happy hour includes pitchers of sangria. And sangria means entertaining with ease. Kick back, relax, chat, and giggle. Prepare simple snacks, have an extra pitcher on deck, and let loose as the long day fades and the hot sun relents.

Creating sangria offers infinite possibilities. Typically, it is a potion consisting of wine, fruit, and spirits. This one, a strawberry rhubarb concoction, is oh so delicious.

METHOD: Mix the sugar and the water, and bring the mixture to a boil. Add two stalks of diced rhubarb (no roots or leaves), and let it cool to room temperature. If rhubarb is not your thing, use ginger and peppercorns instead.

Into a pitcher, add the orange and lemon slices and a couple of handfuls of strawberries. I also throw in a handful of mulberries. If you want to jazz it up, add a shot or two of rum. I like a spiced rum, but light or dark are also lovely. Add the chardonnay and sparkling blood orange San Pellegrino (tonic or seltzer work fine as a substitute). Add the orange peach mango juice.

I garnished the pitcher with a sprig of gloriously aromatic lemon verbena. You may want to have a bowl of fruit on hand to go in the glasses before pouring in the sangria.

MULLED WINE

1 bottle (750mL [25.4 fl. oz.]) red wine (I choose something hearty, like a Cabernet, Zinfandel, or Merlot)

¼ c. (50mL) brandy

Few cloves

1 or 2 cinnamon sticks

½ to 1 tsp. (2.5 to 5mL) fresh ginger (use a little more if it's dried)

Pinch of allspice

Few peppercorns

⅛ to ¼ lb. (0.07 to 0.1kg) (about ⅓ to ½ c.) honey or sugar to taste

Zest and juice of 2 oranges, reserve some zest to garnish

1 apple, cut in wedges (I like the tartness of a Granny Smith)

Like sangria, mulled wine is a classic, and there are infinite variations. Most are served warm, a combination of a deep red wine or port, strong warming spices, zesty citrus, and a little something sweet. Many are fortified with brandy or rum. Mulled wine is traditionally served around the winter holidays. A survey of ancient and modern recipes from Victorian England, Germany, Austria (it translates to glow-wine!), the Nordic countries, Netherlands, France, Bulgaria, and many others reveal very similar recipes and ingredients. This recipe is lovely, and if there is a little left over, use it to cook something scrumptious.

METHOD: Mix all the ingredients together and gently heat the mixture—but do not even get close to boiling. Stir occasionally, and serve after about 20 minutes. Garnish with some of the zest and an apple slice. Honestly, though, this is such a warm and delicious treat, it'll be well received any way you serve it.

Chapter 4
ENJOYING YOUR WINE

Now that you have made and bottled your wine, we'll explore
serving, pairing, sharing, and enjoying it. You'll learn about
different wine glasses, serving temperatures, best food and wine
pairings, and how to properly taste a wine. You'll also meet a chef
who shares delicious ideas for food and wine pairings. By the
time you've finished the chapter, you'll feel like a real expert, even
if you started out with little to no knowledge about enjoying wine.

ACCESSORIES

You might find very nice accessories at thrift shops and yard sales for serving and enjoying wines. Some of the treasures that I've collected personally include a terra cotta crock that is great at keeping a bottle of chardonnay chilled on our picnic table, decanters, ice buckets, the perfect picnic basket, and corkscrews. I've also collected some random kitchen gadgets that have been converted to winemaking tools—and beloved, well-used ones at that! Keep an eye out when you are out and about; this stuff is great to have for entertaining or to take along to special occasions.

Wine glasses

One of the most obvious things necessary to enjoying your wine is the wine glass. A multitude of differently shaped glasses have been designed to deliver specific results. The shape of the glass impacts how you perceive the aroma or bouquet of the wine and makes a real difference to how wines taste. Using a thin, clear, colorless glass allows a wine's color and brilliance to shine through. The inside of the glass (the bowl) should allow a circular movement to aerate and reveal the wines' intrinsic characteristics. Traditionally, wine glasses have stems to make it easier to hold them and to keep your hands off of the actual glass part, keeping chilled wines cooler longer and maintaining the wines visual brilliance by avoiding fingerprints and smudges.

The chart on page 157 illustrates five different sizes and shapes of glasses and their functions. Basically, the larger the bowl is, the better the aromas can circulate, which is perfect for reds, since they need more time and air to open up. For whites, use smaller and narrower glasses to concentrate fruit tones and aromas, reducing surface area and in turn the rate of oxidation (which can hide the delicate nuances of white wines). Champagne and sparkling wines are served in narrow, delicately tapered flutes. This shape creates an even smaller surface area, which helps to keep the bubbles intact. A dessert wine glass should be smaller. This helps the wine to go to the back of the mouth so the sweetness does not overwhelm.

Some accessories for enjoying wine that you might find useful include picnic baskets with wine compartments, an ice bucket, a wine opener, and a terra cotta crock to keep chilled wine cool.

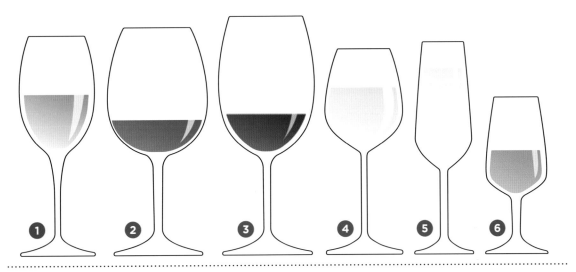

GUIDE TO WINE GLASSES

Glass Shape	Type of Wine	Size of Bowl	Details
1	Standard (any)	Medium size and shape	If you only buy one kind of wine glass for drinking all your wines, buy this.
2	Light Red	Large, very round	Very shallow fill.
3	Bold Red	Large, round	Shallow fill.
4	White	Small, narrow	Fill to a higher level.
5	Sparkling/champagne	Small, very narrow	Fill close to brim.
6	Dessert	Very small, narrow	Fill half way.

A minimalist at heart, I'm a big fan of stemless glasses—love the form, love the function. I try not to get too carried away with needing five varieties of glasses for red wine, but I will tell you my very favorite specialty wine glass is the sipper port glass. Drinking out of that little glass, straw-like tube is just plain fun. The wine you drink is from the bottom of the glass, so you get the least oxidized portion first. I was a skeptic at first, but after a few sips from the bottom, I could not resist taking a sip from the top. I was in awe to discover the notable difference in taste.

My final word on glassware is that you want to be certain to clean all glassware well and rinse, rinse, and rinse again, so nothing taints the next wine you pour into the glass.

Temperature

The other key consideration in serving and appreciating wine is temperature. Just like the glass, temperature can have a very big impact. If a wine is too hot, the alcohol can dominate. If a wine is too cold, it mutes the flavors and aromas. Dry whites, rosés, dessert, and sparkling wines are best between 40 to 50°F (5 to 10°C). Light fruity reds and full-bodied whites are best between 50 to 60°F (10 to 15°C).

QUICK GUIDE TO WINE TEMPERATURES

Type of Wine	Ideal Temperature
Dry whites, rosés, dessert, sparkling wines	40–50°F (5–10°C)
Light fruity reds, full-bodied wines	50–60°F (10–15°C)
Full-bodied reds, ports	60–65°F (15–18°C)

Finally, full-bodied reds and ports are best between 60 to 65°F (15 to 18°C). Mostly you'll want to put your white wines in the refrigerator for an hour or two; if it's a full-bodied white, 45 minutes will do. If your reds get warm, chill them for 15 to 20 minutes. Chill champagne for 2 hours and dessert wines for 1½ hours; serve port at room temperature. Need another cold bottle but have none on hand? Feel free to try this trick at home: put your bottle in a bucket with ice, water, and a handful of salt, and it'll be chilled in 5 to 6 minutes.

Decanting and aerating

Decisions also need to be made about how long in advance you'll want to open wines, and if you'll want to aerate or decant. Opening a red early to let it breathe allows the wine to warm and mix with the air, opens up the aromas and softens or mellows the flavors, and lets the fruit shine through. A typical amount of air time is 15 to 20 minutes; a young wine might need an hour.

Pouring and swirling the wine also serve to aerate it. There is a fascinating array of gadgets to aerate wine, things you pour through, pour over, special funnels, whisks, items that bubble air through, even metallic discs with embedded crystals that aerate and harmonize the wine. As a general rule, the more dense and concentrated a wine is, the more it will benefit from aeration and the longer it will last. Remember, however, that you won't want to aerate older wines, because you can end up going too far and missing the aromas and complexities. I'm a big fan of comparisons: try pulling a cork and tasting the wine before it breathes at all; then, try it with minor aeration, then with major aeration, and note the differences.

Decanting is a great idea if you have a wine that has sediment in it. Pour the bulk of the wine from the bottle to the decanter and leave the sludge behind in the bottle. The other purpose for decanting is to aid aeration. If you decide you are going to decant, make sure the bottle has been sitting upright for a day or two to allow the sediment to settle to the bottom. Use a bright light to see how much sediment you have, and decant very slowly, going even slower as you get near the bottom.

HOST A WINE PARTY

One of the best ways to enjoy your wine is to host a party. You can have a casual party, a fancy party, a large party, a small party—whatever suits your mood.

One of my favorite parties to host is a wine, cheese, and chocolate "potluck." Here's how I do it. Set the scene with some beautiful flowers, petals strewn about, candles and tiki torches, and some gorgeous veggies straight from the market. The simplicity of fresh fruits, dried fruits, and vegetables will serve as a perfect complement to whatever cheeses, chocolates, and wines your guests choose to bring. Have a few of your favorite wines on hand and add theirs to the spread as they arrive. Follow the advice found in this chapter in deciding what order to open the wines, but leave the opener handy should anyone have a hankering for something out of order. Roll with it, and really savor how the flavors combine. This night is meant to delight the senses and invoke much laughter. Wine, cheese, and chocolate: it will be a very special and memorable occasion.

Pouring order

If you are going to be pouring multiple wines, pour them in a proper order. The general flow goes: white before red, dry before sweet, light body before heavy body, all wines before fortified wines, sparkling first, and young before old.

Look, smell, and taste

Tasting wine in a more analytic way will help to deepen your appreciation for the wines you make and all the wines that you taste. The process is look, smell, and taste—pretty straightforward. It truly is the combination of smell and taste that allow you to discern flavor. Here are some basic suggestions to start you on your way.

Remember that using a sparkling, clean, crystal clear wine glass is ideal.

When you look at your wine, observe the color as well as the clarity of it. Look with something white in the background (use a napkin or a tablecloth if you don't have a white wall handy). Tilt the glass away from you, notice how clear it is (or, in the case of my peach wine from a few years back, how clear it is not). Really try to explore the color. Yes, red wine is red, but red wine can be so many shades of red. It can be ruby, purple, or maroon; it can be tawny, which is a brownish, or brick-like red. Same with a white: look beyond white to pale yellow, a tinge of green, straw-like, golden, amber. Notice also if the wine seems clear or cloudy, dull or brilliant. Is there sediment or floaters? Really take it in. You'll learn that older wines begin to darken and show those tawny brownish tones. Swirl the glass and look again. Does it change at all?

After you've taken a good look, swirl the wine in your glass for ten seconds and then take a big whiff. Swirl it some more, and stick your nose down into the glass and really deeply inhale. Notice again what you smell, play with it, say any word that comes to mind.

At last, enjoy your first little taste. Take just a tiny sip and start to sniff it on the way in; notice what you taste. Consider if you notice alcohol, and if it seems sweet, or tart and acidic, and tannic. You'll start to notice the wine's taste: the fruits, the flavors. After your sip, notice how the wine "finishes." Does the flavor linger? Really take some time to notice what the lasting impression is and if it makes you want to go right back for another sip.

FOOD AND WINE PAIRING

There's no better way to enjoy your wine than when it's paired with a delicious meal or dessert. Let's take a look at some guidelines on food and wine pairings.

Food and wine have a long, long history of being served together, and, essentially, winemaking and culinary traditions have evolved together. The goal is simply to choose wines that complement the food you are serving them with so that during the meal, when you are going back and forth from food to wine, you can enjoy, appreciate, and savor the essence of both.

If you are enjoying an elaborate meal with several courses, serve your wines according to these simple guidelines:

- Dry before sweet
- White before red
- Young before old
- Simple before complex
- Light before heavy

When choosing a wine for a course or a meal, balance the wine's characteristics with the food's characteristics:

- Richer, more robust foods pair best with heavier, fuller flavored wines.
- Delicate foods go with delicate wines.
- Spicy foods pair well with sweeter wines.
- Grilled or charred foods pair well with oaked wines.
- Salty foods go with sweeter wines.
- And dessert should be served with sweet wines.

Above all, remember that food and wine pairing is a very subjective thing. Everyone has a different palate.

Also, even some of the old standard advice (red wine with beef and lamb, white wine with chicken and fish) needs to be tempered by saying that if your chicken has a rich sauce, it may pair better with a medium-bodied red wine.

This pairing is all about like with like. The dish, east coast razor clams with arugula and preserved lemon pesto, garlic, semolina pasta and chili soffrito, has very clean, bright, and citrusy flavors. To complement those flavors, pair with a wine that shares similar characteristics, like any high acid, clean, crisp, Italian white wine such as Italian Pinot Grigio, or CA Sauvignon Blanc.

Wine and Food Pairing Guru

~ TAYLOR MASON ~

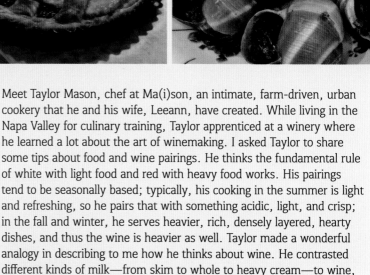

Meet Taylor Mason, chef at Ma(i)son, an intimate, farm-driven, urban cookery that he and his wife, Leeann, have created. While living in the Napa Valley for culinary training, Taylor apprenticed at a winery where he learned a lot about the art of winemaking. I asked Taylor to share some tips about food and wine pairings. He thinks the fundamental rule of white with light food and red with heavy food works. His pairings tend to be seasonally based; typically, his cooking in the summer is light and refreshing, so he pairs that with something acidic, light, and crisp; in the fall and winter, he serves heavier, rich, densely layered, hearty dishes, and thus the wine is heavier as well. Taylor made a wonderful analogy in describing to me how he thinks about wine. He contrasted different kinds of milk—from skim to whole to heavy cream—to wine, thinking of them in terms of having weight. Dessert wine is a cream, and a thin light white wine is a skim milk. His final thought—and this comes as no surprise, given his passion for sourcing his own ingredients in the purest way possible—"If it grows together, it goes together."

▶ Taylor Mason, the talented chef at Ma(i)son in Lancaster, Pennsylvania, provides expert advice on food and wine pairing.

THE FINAL WORD

I hope I've been able to communicate the reverence I have for the art of winemaking. I hope you've glimpsed the joy it has brought to my life and the awe that I have for the magic of transforming the juice of a grape or other fruit into a complex, aromatic, and enjoyable elixir. And I hope this book will inspire and nurture the winemaker in you. I wish for you the creation and enjoyment of beautiful wine.

This quote by H. Warner Allen says so much about the experience of appreciating wine:

"As the last drops were being sipped, a guest, savoring preciously every fragrance, said with unaffected humility: 'When I drink wines such as these, I ask myself what merit I have acquired that I should be allowed to experience such beauty.'"

ABOUT THE AUTHOR

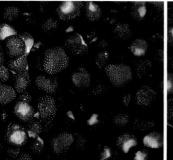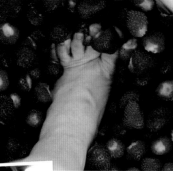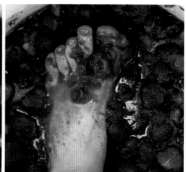

I've always loved the whole ritual of the stomping of the grapes. As I was about to begin crushing these beautiful strawberries, I could not resist making a photograph of "stomping the strawberries."

When I'm not dreaming up wine recipes and making wine, I'm often found growing and questing for winemaking ingredients, making photographs, tending to my bees, and lobbying and educating on their behalf. I'm thankful for a career as a commercial photographer that has afforded me time and space for abundant creative endeavors. A few years ago I created BeeBees All Naturals, a "beeautiful" business that grew out of a calling to beekeeping. While renovating a 1830s mill that serves as studio, gallery, and home to BeeBees, I began what has turned into a ten-year apprenticeship with a stonemason, a pursuit that has taught me more about patience and life than ever I could have imagined.

After working a long harvest season helping in a commercial winery, I happily returned to the simple pure artistry and meditation that winemaking is for me. I'm thankful that in my home in Lancaster, Pennsylvania, I'm surrounded by some top-notch vineyards and wineries, fine enology training opportunities, and an incredible community of winemakers.

Come visit me on Facebook at:
www.facebook.com/pages/The-Winemaker/518112508227912.

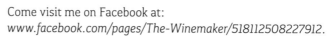

SUPPLIERS

Adams County Winery, *www.adamscountywinery.com*
Adventures in Homebrewing, *www.homebrewing.org*
The Beer Place Homebrew and Winemaking Supply, *www. facebook.com/TheBeerPlaceHomebrewAndWinemakingSupply*
BlueStem Winery, *www.bluestemwine.com*
Brewcraft USA*, *www.brewcraftusa.com*
BSG Handcraft*, *www.bsghandcraft.com*
E. C. Kraus, *www.eckraus.com*
Fall Bright, *www.fallbright.com*

*Wholesale only

F.H. Steinbart, *www.fhsteinbart.com*
Home Sweet Homebrew, *www.homesweethomebrew.com*
Keystone Homebrew Supply, *www.keystonehomebrew.com*
Lancaster Homebrew, *www.lancasterhomebrew.com*
LD Carlson*, *www.ldcarlson.com*
Midwest Supplies, *www.midwestsupplies.com*
MoreFlavor!, *www.moreflavor.com*
Northern Brewer, *www.northernbrewer.com*
Presque Isle Wine Cellars, *www.piwine.com*
Scotzin Bros., *www.scotzinbros.com*
Wine Making Superstore, *www.winemakingsuperstore.com*
Other resources: *www.winemaking.jackkeller.net/shops.asp*

INDEX

Note: Page numbers in *italics* indicate recipes.